CHICAGO IN

TRANSITION

previous page
This aerial view of metropolitan Chicago looks northeast along
the South Branch of the Chicago River during the 1930s. Many of
the river's tributaries have since been filled in. Downtown can
be identified as the concentration of tall buildings in the distance
(Chicago Aerial Survey Co. Photo, Eric Bronsky Collection).

Edited by Eric Bronsky, Neal Samors and Jennifer Samors
Produced by Eric Bronsky and Neal Samors
Designed by Sam Silvio, Silvio Design, Inc.
Printed in Canada by Friesens Corporation

ISBN 0-9797892-0-6

Front Cover
Randolph Street, looking west towards State Street on
January 15, 1933 (courtesy of the Chicago Transit Authority).

Back Cover
A contemporary view of the same stretch of Randolph
Street, photographed from Marshall Field's 7th floor on
December 26, 2005. Except for the Oriental Theatre, now
officially known as Ford Center for the Performing Arts,
everything else has changed (Eric Bronsky photo).

For more information on this book as well as the authors'
other works, visit www.chicagosbooks.com or email the
authors at EBronsky@aol.com or NSamors@comcast.net.

Table of Contents

8   Preface

10   Acknowledgments

12   Foreword By Joel Daly

22   Part I—The Rise Skyward

64   Part II—Two Challenging Decades

138   Part III—The Construction Boom

202   Part IV—Renaissance

240   Part V—Epilogue

250   Interviewee Biographies

251   Photo Index

252   Subject Index

Preface

If you could ride a time machine back to downtown Chicago of fifty years ago, what an amazingly different place you'd find. The observation deck on the top floor of the Prudential Building, then Chicago's tallest building, was downtown's most popular tourist attraction. First-run Cinemascope and Cinerama features were playing at movie palaces on Randolph and State Streets. Palatial department stores like Marshall Field's, Mandel Brothers and The Fair lined both sides of State Street. You could enjoy dinner at restaurants like Blackhawk, Fritzel's and Henrici's or snack at Woolworth's lunch counter, then spend the night at moderately-priced hotels like the Morrison, LaSalle or Sherman House. Chicago was the railroad capital of the USA and you could ride a train in style directly into downtown from almost every part of the country.

The institutions that were such a vibrant a part of our everyday lives fifty or a hundred years ago are now mostly vanished or else changed beyond recognition. Today there are few intercity trains left to take you downtown, but once there you'll find Millennium Park, Macy's, Petterino's, Old Navy, LaSalle Bank Theatre, McDonald's, CVS Pharmacy, and the Hard Rock Hotel. Fifty years from now? Well, one thing is certain—almost everything will have changed again.

Our inspiration for writing a book about the evolution of downtown Chicago through the years was spurred by very recent events. Within a two-year period, three prominent downtown institutions synonymous with Chicago vanished or changed. Marshall Field's flagship store was sold and converted to Macy's. The 107-year-old Berghoff Restaurant closed, opening a few months later under a different name and concept. Finally, Carson Pirie Scott shuttered their landmark store at State and Madison.

Like other native Chicagoans weaned on local icons since early childhood, our reaction to these changes was a mix of anger, sadness and nostalgia...but more importantly, we felt a sense of irrevocable loss at the prospect of places, pastimes and things long familiar to us vanishing perhaps forever.

So, we set out to preserve our memory of these fine places in tangible form. Photography being one of Eric's passions, he went straight to work with his digital camera. To facilitate sharing some of his favorite photos with friends he started writing e-mail narratives, but when the size and scope of these kept growing and expanding, Eric and Neal began to contemplate combining text and images into a more lasting document.

Chicago's colorful history has always fascinated both authors and their personal libraries are bulging with photographs and books that they have collected through the years. In addition, Neal had authored or co-authored several earlier books about the city including *The Old Chicago Neighborhood, Chicago in the Fifties* and *Chicago in the Sixties.* Eric was one of the key interviewees in the books about the '50s and the '60s. The proverbial "one-thing-led-to-another" scenario led to both authors agreeing to collaborate on this book about downtown Chicago in transition

This book is not intended as a concise or detailed chronological history of downtown Chicago. Instead, it focuses on the continuum of change across many decades as witnessed by several Chicagoans and documented by camera. Through the words and images presented on these pages, we aim to convey a sense of time and place based more on firsthand experience than third-person accounts. We truly enjoyed assembling this record of Chicago's dynamic past, and we invite you to share in the fun and nostalgia as we travel together back in time.

Eric Bronsky and Neal Samors

Sheldon "Shey" Fields

Downtown Chicago may be dominated by big businesses, but entrepreneurs who eke out a living on the streets are also a part of the city's fabric. In the late fifties a candid photographer with a rather clunky camera used to frequent Randolph Street. As you approached him he would snap your photo and then hand you a small brown envelope with a number stamped on it. Address the envelope and give it back to him with a quarter, and several days later you would receive in the mail a small and somewhat blurry black & white print.

My parents and I encountered him several times. We wouldn't take the envelope, but this never seemed to faze the photographer who was always pleasant and smiling.

After a year or so, the candid photographer disappeared. But he and I were destined to meet again. In 1987 he became my father-in-law.

Sheldon Fields, a family man and lifelong Chicagoan who preferred to be called Shey, went on to greater entrepreneurial success as a business owner and manager. Big businesses may have shaped the city, but the warmth, energy and can-do attitude of people like Shey helped to make Chicago a better place.

Eric Bronsky

Harry and Bessie Samors

My paternal grandparents, Harry and Bessie Samors, came to America in the late 1800s from Russia and settled in Chicago on the city's West Side. They married in 1902 and were wed for 72 years before passing away, within six weeks of each other, in 1974.

During their years in Chicago they lived not only on the West Side, but also in South Shore on the South Side and Edgewater on the North Side. One of their greatest pleasures, other than being White Sox fans, was to travel downtown on the IC or the "L" to visit the city's magnificent department stores, movie palaces and restaurants.

Some of my clearest memories were those times when my parents, sister and I would meet my grandparents downtown in order to have a delicious dinner at Henrici's Restaurant on Randolph Street. It was a magnificent place with great food and wonderful service.

I warmly dedicate this book to Harry and Bessie's memory.

Neal Samors

Acknowledgments

We want to express our sincerest gratitude to Joel Daly for writing the excellent foreword to *Downtown Chicago in Transition*. It provides readers with a remembrance of some of the important changes that occurred in the downtown area during the latter half of the twentieth century and helps to set the framework of the book.

Also, special acknowledgment to the organizations that provided access to their outstanding photo collections and to the individuals who gave so much time in support of our effort. They include Ron Theel and Trina Higgins of the *Chicago Sun-Times*; Bruce Moffat and Joyce Shaw of the Chicago Transit Authority; Rob Medina and Gary Johnson of the Chicago History Museum; Bradley D. Cook, Curator of the Charles W. Cushman Collection at Indiana University; Robert S. McGonigal, Editor of *Classic Trains* Magazine; and Lorna Donley, Morag Walsh and Teresa G. Yoder of Harold Washington Library. In addition, our deepest thanks to Jerome R. Butler, Artistic Events by Carlyn Berghoff Catering, Ed Halstead, George E. Kanary, Mary Robinson Kalista, and the Wien-Criss Archive for providing beautiful photographs from their collections. We want to express our deepest gratitude to Ann Roth and Bob Vorachek at Don Roth's Blackhawk Restaurant for allowing us to use a group of photographs from the restaurant's collection. Also, special thanks to Josephine Baskin Minow for connecting the authors with some of the key interviewees who participated in the development of this book, and to Jeff Wien for volunteering many hours of his time assisting us with CTA's photo collection.

The authors want to express appreciation and acknowledgment to the following individuals whose oral histories provided us with the rich details concerning their memories of a downtown Chicago in transition. Their remembrances are personal, poignant, vibrant and humorous, and provide the depth of experiences described in this book. They include: Jerome R. Butler, Michael Demetrio, Jerry Field, Marshall Field V, Myles Jarrow, Gary Johnson, Bernard Judge, Mary Robinson Kalista, George E. Kanary, Mitch Markovitz, Robert Markovitz, Kay Mayer, James McDonough, Paul Meincke, Josephine Baskin Minow, James O'Connor, Potter Palmer IV, Ann Roth, J.J. Sedelmaier, and David Welch.

"[Chicago] was a blank canvas,
certainly from an architectural standpoint,
and its personality was defined by
the spirit necessary for its resurrection."
J.J. Sedelmaier

Foreword By Joel Daly

*"…On State Street, that great street, I just gotta say,
they do things they don't do on Broadway"*

When I arrived on State Street on a hot August day in 1967,
I felt I had hit "the big time". Let's face it, they don't sing songs about
Cleveland! I would stand during the dinner hour at the entrance of
WLS-TV at State and Lake and watch the passing parade of exuberant
pedestrians—rich, poor, white and black.

Next door to our studios was the State Lake Theater, later to be converted into a studio for Oprah. Fritzel's Restaurant, home of Kup's original "Booth Number One," was kitty-corner. If you jaywalked (and everyone in Chicago did), you could get the best corned beef sandwich in town at Elfman's, presided over by Joel Elfman, the self-proclaimed "Prince of State Street."

Next to Elfman's was the Chicago Theater, where Bob Hope and so many others performed. Down the block, on the corner of State and Randolph, was Walgreen's from where we used to broadcast the New Year's Eve Party—this was the epicenter of the city. We put a camera on the roof of that building and the temperature was always below zero. One New Year's Eve the crowd got overzealous and pushed our on-the-scene reporter, Art Hellyer, through a plate-glass window. Art's back was never the same. Like so many other State Street institutions, the New Year's Eve celebration eventually moved uptown.

On the same block where Art fell were Jack Cohen's Pawn Shop—a veritable treasure trove—and Orange Julius. These have been replaced by a residence for students of the Art Institute, the Gene Siskel Film Center and Border's Bookstore. Across from Walgreen's was the famous Marshall Field's Department Store, where people met each other "under the clock."

Outside our studios you could feel the rumble of the subway underneath the sidewalk. The grates that ventilated the tunnel emitted air that was a constant 65 degrees, which made it feel cool in the summer and warm in the winter. Overhead was the screech of the "L," which took you to within a block of Wrigley Field or Comiskey Park.

It was an exciting time to be in the center of the city. But then our toddlin' town grew quiet. The atmosphere changed. People who could afford it fled to the suburbs. Sales dropped and theatres closed. In an effort to revive State Street the city turned it into a mall, with only buses and delivery trucks allowed on the roadway. I broadcast the opening ceremonies in a live report atop the State Lake Theatre marquee. The mall was a bust, bathed in diesel fumes.

The greasy-spoon restaurants and arcades across from Field's were torn down, further reducing the character of State Street. The resulting vacancy, called Block 37, simply left a dirty hole at State and Randolph. It stood vacant for nearly 20 years except for a summertime art show and a wintertime ice-rink.

Entertainment from a grandstand on Block 37 regularly showcased Joel Daly and the Sundowners. This was a country music trio with whom I worked for nearly 40 years. They were the house band for the Double R Bar Ranch—the Ranch for short—located first in a basement on Madison Street, then below Plato's Place at Randolph and Dearborn. The Double R featured 38 varieties of chili and was a watering hole for Loop workers and visiting out-of-town celebrities. Country music stars regularly sat in with the Sundowners.

But the times and tunes changed! Wieboldt's moved out, Marshall Field's became Macy's, and Carson Pirie Scott was closed to become, at last report, a first-floor grocery store. Walgreen's is "going condo." And around the corner, where we used to listen to the finest jazz, the London House was converted into a Burger King.

Yet the city continues to evolve with new buildings and new people, as it has for decades. And yes …

"Bet your bottom dollar, you'll lose the blues in Chicago… Chicago…Chicago my home town."

STATE LAKE
"THE ROBE"
CINEMASCOPE
STEREOPHONIC SOUND
MIDWEST
PREMIERE
Oxford
Van Heusen
SHIRTS
Pierre Savoree
HATS
SUBWAY
USE THIS PLEASE
PUT RUBBISH HERE
BUREAU OF SANITATION
NO PARKING
AIR RAID SHELTER

By 2007 the building at 190 North State was dwarfed by surrounding office towers, and the State Lake Theatre had been converted to studio space for WLS-TV (Eric Bronsky photo).

Northeast corner of Dearborn and Randolph in 1910
(courtesy of the Chicago Transit Authority).

Northeast corner of Dearborn and Randolph in 2007
(Eric Bronsky photo).

Michigan Avenue looking south from Washington in 1946 (courtesy of the Chicago Transit Authority).

Michigan Avenue looking south from Washington in 2007 (Eric Bronsky photo).

East side of Wabash Avenue looking north from Washington in 1954,
shortly after new mercury vapor streetlights were installed.
As published in the *Chicago Sun-Times*. Photographer: Joe Kordick
(Copyright 1954 by Chicago Sun-Times, Inc. Reprinted with permission).

East side of Wabash Avenue looking north from Washington in 2007.
The mercury vapor lights of the 50s were replaced with replicas
of old-style street lamps (Eric Bronsky photo).

Garland Court looking north towards Randolph c. 1920
(courtesy Chicago History Museum)

Garland Court looking north towards Randolph in 2007
(Eric Bronsky photo).

PART I
THE RISE SKYWARD
1870s-1920s

An Urban Center in Transition

Over the centuries, a river gradually changes course because its currents erode rock and sediment from one part of the bank and deposit the detritus elsewhere. Downtown Chicago has ebbed, flowed, and changed course in similar fashion. Tides of people enter in the morning and depart at night; businesses open, flourish, and then fade; and obsolete buildings and infrastructure are renewed or replaced. But unlike a river, the yardstick that we use to measure change over time in this urban center is calibrated in units significantly smaller than centuries.

Nature and the elements play a minuscule role in determining the course of downtown Chicago's evolution. Perhaps we should credit the main impetus for change to socioeconomic factors in the broadest terms, but we also need to identify and understand the various events and trends that worked together and disparately to shape downtown.

Planning and development: The seeds for downtown as we know it today were sown over 150 years ago on the approximate site of the city's original settlement at the mouth of the Chicago River. Entrepreneurial and political forces determined land usage from the start. In an era before such visionaries as Daniel Burnham, planners paid scant attention to esthetics and congestion. But as downtown property became more desirable and increased in value, these concerns melded into sharp focus. Ordinances were instituted to effect ever-higher standards for safety and livability. Thus, downtown gradually evolved from a post-fire boomtown to a metropolis where every major new project is scrupulously choreographed by a retinue of urban planners, architects, engineers, environmentalists, government entities, and civic groups.

Sociological: The influence of various ethnic groups has always been evident. In earlier years a large percentage of the work force consisted of European immigrants—many businesses were owned by or else catered to them. Then, successive generations of American-born citizenry formed a large middle class that predominated for many decades. Ethnic and cultural diversity would return to downtown many years later with the expansion of Chicago's African-American, Asian, and Hispanic populations.

Architectural: Chicago's role as a leader in the evolution of the modern skyscraper has been well documented. There were four distinct periods of commercial building design that began with downtown's rise from the ashes following the 1871 Great Fire: 6- to 8-story loft buildings, European-influenced skyscrapers competing with the Chicago school, modernism, and postmodernism.

Transportation: As industry and technology progressed, land transportation evolved from animal power to rail to rubber tire. The importance of the Chicago River as a thoroughfare declined through the decades, and although the modes of passenger and goods transport have changed, the geographic travel corridors that have linked downtown with the city and suburbs have remained essentially unchanged for, in most cases, well over a century.

Commerce and Industry: By the dawn of the twentieth century, downtown had become the city's main wholesale marketplace and light manufacturing district as well as a mecca for retail shopping. The first two activities were gradually displaced by urban renewal and a burgeoning service industry. Many retail businesses, together with shoppers, eventually migrated to more upscale North Michigan Avenue and suburban shopping malls. Most of the locally owned stores, restaurants, and hotels that remained downtown either went out of business or were taken over by national chains.

Culture and Entertainment: Chicago's early investors and developers brought a surprisingly sophisticated appreciation of the fine arts to what had begun as a frontier town in the Northwest Territory. The visual as well as performing arts have always had a presence here, but in recent years these have benefited from renewed interest and investment. Venues for stage performances evolved from seedy vaudeville houses to ornate movie palaces which, after several decades of neglect, were gloriously restored.

Environment: Downtown of the mid-nineteenth century was infested with vermin, riddled with disease epidemics, and reeking of filth and contaminants. Heroic actions by Chicago's leaders and planners were needed to reverse decades of neglect and poor planning. Over time, the quality of life downtown dramatically improved.

Two factors relating to downtown Chicago's development and growth should be noted. First, ongoing urban projects that began with the raising of downtown street grades in the 1850s and continued through the present time have invariably met with stormy protests from the people who would be inconvenienced or displaced. Yet such projects almost always ended with accolades from many more that were able to benefit from the improvements. A key fringe benefit has been enhanced property values.

Of far greater concern, though, is the perennial controversy over whether specific entities should be managed by public or private enterprise. In theory, our society defers decision-making to government, but in reality the private sector, ranging from entrepreneurs to giant national conglomerates, has been influential enough to alter Chicago's course. Some arguments in favor of privatizing certain city services appeared to have merit, while the downside has been reduced public participation in decision-making.

Carl Sandburg, in his famous 1916 poem "Chicago," used words like stormy, husky, brawling, wicked, crooked, brutal, coarse, and fierce to describe the city. Fortunately, downtown Chicago gradually transcended the literal description conveyed by his words. Whereas big-city downtowns elsewhere were turning into ghost towns, this urban center managed to survive through innovation and by adapting to a changing world. It is Chicago's unique blend of geography, heritage, leadership, and civic pride that has made its downtown a very special place.

Rebuilding After the Fire

Perhaps the only positive aspect of the conflagration that destroyed most of the central city in 1871 was that it gave civic leaders, planners, and businesses a clean slate upon which to start anew. New buildings, though rushed to completion, were grander, sturdier, and more fireproof than their predecessors. However, urban planning did not exist as we know it today. Speculative land buyers sought to make the most of their investments by abutting building facades up to the edge of the sidewalk in a solid line. A sea of boxy buildings averaging six to eight stories tall soon filled up every city block, and the only open space remaining was streets and sidewalks.

Further spread of downtown's rapid growth was constrained by both natural and man-made boundaries. On the north and west were the Chicago River Main and South Branches, respectively. Just east of Michigan Avenue were the tracks of the Illinois Central Railroad. To the south was a rapidly growing complex of railroad passenger depots, rail yards, and freight houses. So the only practical direction to expand downtown was upward, and the advent of the skyscraper and the passenger elevator during the 1880s certainly made that possible.

Downtown's original core of commercial activity had centered around the mouth of the Chicago River, but as the increasing use of railroads to transport raw materials and goods led to a gradual decline in river traffic, this core gradually shifted southward and slightly to the west. Left behind was the wholesale produce market that paralleled the river's Main Branch along South Water Street. As Chicago evolved into a manufacturing center during the 1880s, factory buildings rose adjacent to the river and the railroads.

Even before the earliest skyscrapers rose, the pattern of commercial geography that is familiar to Chicagoans today was being patched together. First and foremost, Chicago pioneered the development of the department store. These giant stores together with other prestigious retail businesses lined both sides of State Street, which not surprisingly was touted as "the greatest shopping street in the world." Taverns and vaudeville houses sprang up on State south of the main retail area. A burgeoning theatre district along Randolph Street overflowed onto intersecting streets. Several cultural institutions called South Michigan Boulevard home. Just one block to the west, companies that manufactured and sold furniture, musical instruments, and art supplies colonized Wabash Avenue. A jewelry district emerged at Wabash and Madison, and financial institutions sprang up along a several block stretch of LaSalle Street.

The arrival of cable cars in the 1880s and elevated trains in the 1890s spurred business by providing a more practical means for people from outlying neighborhoods to travel downtown. Retail businesses established their storefronts as close as possible to these transportation corridors. The main hub of the surface routes was the area bounded by a cable car loop on Madison, Wabash, Lake, and State, so naturally retailers preferred to be within that area. Construction of the Loop "L" in 1897 further expanded the perceived boundaries of the main Loop retail district to Wabash, Lake, Wells, and Van Buren.

But it was two pivotal events that truly set the course for the future growth and evolution of downtown. First, the World's Columbian Exposition of 1893 imbued Chicago's leaders with an awareness of the city's place in the world and a sense of optimism about the future. The classical European style buildings that were built for the "White City" spurred a resurgence of traditional architecture, which would pose a challenge to the far more innovative "Chicago school" design of downtown buildings over the next three decades.

Then in 1909, the Commercial Club of Chicago commissioned architects Daniel Burnham and Edward Bennett to prepare the ambitious *Plan of Chicago*, which cohesively integrated buildings, parks, cultural attractions, and transportation into an idealistic plan to "bring order out of chaos" and ultimately improve living conditions. This, the first comprehensive plan for the growth and development of any large city, arguably had a more profound influence over the long-term improvement and beautification of downtown than anything since. The preservation of Chicago's lakefront as a parkland is the most visible result of the *Plan's* foresight.

"The Fair Store had the finest toy department in all Chicago, bar none! It occupied a big space on the eighth floor and blew Marshall Field's right out of the water!"
George E. Kanary

Loft buildings erected after the Great Fire on the southwest corner of
Market and Washington stood where the Civic Opera House would eventually
be built (Eric Bronsky Collection).

Looking north on Michigan Boulevard from Congress in 1910
(courtesy of the Chicago Transit Authority).

The Wurlitzer store on Wabash Avenue between Jackson and Van Buren
(courtesy of the Chicago History Museum, ICHi-16786).

"Marshall Field's provided a
wide range of services to their
customers. For example, if
you wanted to know how to set
a table, you called them;
if you wanted to know how to
address an envelope, you called
them...they were the authorities
on how to do everything."
Ann Roth

Gary T. Johnson

All of my direct ancestors who immigrated to America from Europe managed to end up coming to the Chicago area and staying here. They include settlers from Norway, who first arrived in Chicago in 1853, and German great-great grandparents living here at the time of the Chicago Fire in 1871.

Originally, the Scandinavian and German members of my family lived on the Near North Side, north of the Chicago River. Then, my first immigrant ancestor (Svale Staaleson – in Norwegian), who changed his name to Samuel Larson, built a house on the street then known as Indiana but now named Grand Avenue. The house was located just west of the river, in what we now call West Town. Then, my Scandinavian ancestors went up Milwaukee Avenue through Humboldt Park and Logan Square and out to Norwood Park and Edison Park. I also have some Swedish ancestors who came to Chicago a little later and they lived just south of Irving Park on Albany Avenue. So, my family came to Chicago and stayed here and I've never had an American ancestor who lived anywhere else except this city.

My relatives had jobs that ranged from being a cooper (barrel maker), owner of a store that sold lutefisk (fish preserved in lye), to a great-great grandparent who was a teamster and drove a team to Half Day to haul produce from the truck farms to Chicago's markets. By the twentieth century, the next generation was still doing a lot of the same kinds of things. The teamster's son became a house painter. The daughter of the cooper, who was in her mother's womb during the Great Chicago Fire, became a housewife.

As it turned out, all my relatives survived the fire.

One of my grandfathers, Tom Johnson, was from a Swedish family, and he graduated from the Linné School. He first took a job at the State Bank of Chicago, which was a Swedish-owned bank that began in the Albany Park-Avondale neighborhood. He started in the mailroom, but, within a few years, he became an officer of that bank when he was only in his early 20s. For many immigrants at the time, the standard was an eighth grade education, and working life began early. The State Bank of Chicago built its downtown building on LaSalle Street, just directly across from where the Field Building was built. For many years it was the Exchange National Bank until it became part of LaSalle Bank, then was absorbed into Chase Bank. One of the curiosities about building in the Loop, if you go around and look when buildings were constructed, it seemed to be right at the end of the Roaring '20s. For example, the Continental Bank building went up right before the Depression, so there was a building spurt across the city in the 1920s—right before the crash. My grandfather wound up as a vice president at the First National Bank of Chicago, where he led the construction division and worked with clients such as the Crown family.

left
State Street looking north towards the Chicago River during the
South Water Street Market era (courtesy of the Chicago Transit Authority).

right
Washington Street between Dearborn and Clark, looking west
towards the new City Hall (photograph by W.T. Barnum, courtesy of
the Chicago History Museum, ICHi-20884)

bottom
Looking west on South Water Street from Clark Street in 1920
(courtesy of the Chicago Transit Authority).

Potter Palmer IV

My great grandfather built the Palmer House and gave it to his bride, Bertha, as a wedding present in 1871.

State Street looking north from Adams showing the Palmer House c. 1911 (photographer unknown, courtesy of the Chicago History Museum ICHi-04790).

right
Ladies' entrance to the Palmer House Hotel, 1903 (photograph by *Chicago Daily News*, courtesy of the Chicago History Museum, DN-0001231).

As fate would have it, the original hotel burned down ten days later during the Great Chicago Fire. So, soon after the fire, he began to build the second Palmer House with the use of a personal loan and a new hotel was erected with fireproof rooms. The third Palmer House was built in the mid-1920s, and I know that my grandfather spent some of his time at the hotel contributing to the design and construction of the building. Then, when my father graduated from college in 1932, he worked in the hotel until the outbreak of WWII in 1941 before joining the Navy. He ended up in the Naval Air Force in the Pacific. But, tragically, he died soon after the end of the war, in the fall of 1946. Thus, he never had much of a career. The hotel was actually sold to Conrad Hilton in the late 1940s.

Getting Downtown

To answer the question of what existed first—populated areas or transportation corridors—one needs to look back to a time when the waterways served as the only tangible connection between Chicago and the rest of the world. It was the river that attracted the earliest settlers to what would eventually become Chicago; the young city grew up around the confluence of the Chicago River and Lake Michigan.

Through the decades, the river played a major though gradually diminishing role in the transport of goods and raw materials, but any other use of local waterways tended to be recreational, usually in the form of steamship excursions to resorts around Lake Michigan and, in more recent years, small pleasure craft.

The first railroads were built to transport people and goods between Chicago and other Illinois towns. As the nation's rail network expanded into a transcontinental goliath, speculators and developers who purchased land along the rail corridors leading into Chicago reaped a fortune as their small rural hamlets blossomed into growing communities that were later annexed into the city of Chicago and became its neighborhoods. Further away from the central city, the small towns that sprouted around rail-road stations became Chicago's suburbs. Whereas the only practical ways to travel into the central city had been by stagecoach or on horseback, the trains made it practical to take day trips into downtown for business or shopping.

Chicago's leaders, observing the detrimental effect that dirt and noise from Illinois Central trains were having on adjacent Michigan Avenue properties, prudently vowed to confine subsequent development of rail terminal facilities to the outskirts of downtown. By the turn of the century, there were six major railroad terminals on the fringes of downtown along with several hundred scheduled daily passenger and freight trains to all parts of the country as well as local commuter service.

Hidden far beneath the surface of downtown's streets was an incredible maze of underground freight tunnels that interconnected the various railroad depots with State Street department stores, the post office, basement boiler rooms and warehouses. Through the first half of the twentieth century, a fleet of electric locomotives transported merchandise, mail, coal, and ashes a world apart from the growing street congestion above.

Of course, a local form of transportation was needed to bring Chicagoans downtown. Horse-drawn streetcars gave way to cable cars in the 1880s and a decade later the first electric streetcars were clanging along State Street. In addition to three tunnels beneath the Chicago River, rails were also extended over new movable bridges being built across the river at one-block intervals, facilitating expansion of the network into what was billed as the largest street railway system in the world.

Chicago's first elevated railroad was designed and built to carry passengers between downtown and the World's Columbian Exposition. Then a shrewd businessman with nefarious motives managed to cajole city leaders into permitting construction of elevated lines directly above city streets. When the Loop "L" rose in 1897, it was almost immediately decried as an unsightly blight and a hindrance to downtown's economic development. Notwithstanding, it quickly became the single most vital component of Chicago's public transportation system, a hub that interconnected the routes of four independent elevated lines and

Chicago & NorthWestern Railway station, located at Madison & Canal, opened in 1911 and was demolished in 1984. The Richard B. Ogilvie Transportation Center occupies this site today (Eric Bronsky photo).

below
Grand Central Station (center) was completed in 1890 and
LaSalle Street Station (upper left) in 1903 (Eric Bronsky Collection).

permitted convenient transfers as well as establishing direct physical connections with the major department stores. Who could have imagined that the Loop "L" would eventually become a revered symbol of Chicago?

The electric interurban railroad bridged the gap between long- and short-haul rail travel. Frequent, convenient, and economical service from downtown Chicago to Aurora, Elgin, Milwaukee, and several intermediate communities once shared the tracks with elevated trains in the city. To this day, electric trains to South Bend continue to share former Illinois Central tracks with Metra Electric suburban trains.

Last to arrive was the private automobile. All of the streets leading into downtown were paved by the turn of the century. The new river bridges that were a boon for the streetcar companies also made it much easier for drivers to access downtown from other parts of the city. By the 1920s, private autos had become a significant contributing factor to downtown's congestion and also raised concerns for pedestrian safety. Parking was totally inadequate, and gridlock became the norm at many Loop intersections. Subsequent attempts to relieve downtown streets of vehicular congestion always fell short of success.

Union Station opened in 1925. The concourse (foreground) was demolished in 1968 but the colonnaded Great Hall (background) remains as the last of Chicago's six passenger railroad terminals (Eric Bronsky Collection).

> "Our geographical position at the tip of Lake Michigan, which extends so far south into the USA, makes it necessary to travel through Chicago, and that's why Chicago became the nation's transportation hub."
> *Myles Jarrow*

top
Workmen prepare to pave around the newly rebuilt streetcar tracks at State and Lake in 1942. As published in the *Chicago Sun-Times*. Photographer: Westelin (Copyright 1942 by Chicago Sun-Times, Inc. Reprinted with permission).

center left
Streetcars intermingle with buses, autos and pedestrians at State and Madison in 1931. The Boston Store, whose clock resembled Marshall Field's, is visible at left. A Sears department store occupies the lower floors of that building today (courtesy of the Chicago Transit Authority).

center right
This sharp S-curve at Wabash & Harrison was a part of the original connection between the old South Side "L" and the Loop (Eric Bronsky photo).

bottom
Chicago Surface Lines cars on Clark Street, looking south towards Randolph c. 1930 (courtesy of the Chicago Transit Authority)

top
Chicago's first wooden "L" car, South Side Rapid Transit no. 1 built in 1892, is westbound on Van Buren near Wells. This beautifully restored car is now preserved at the Chicago History Museum (Eric Bronsky photo).

center left
These 1913-era steel "L" cars, viewed at Wabash and Lake, were built with center doors that were not used (William C. Hoffman photo, Wien-Criss Archive).

center right
Market Street Terminal, located on Market Street (later Wacker Drive), was the original terminus of the Lake Street "L." After this route was connected to the Loop "L," a few rush hour trains continued to use this station until it closed in 1948. The Civic Opera House is at left. As published in the *Chicago Sun-Times.* Photographer: Padulo Jr. (Copyright 1938 by Chicago Sun-Times, Inc. Reprinted with permission).

bottom
State Street looking south towards Quincy during subway construction in 1941 (courtesy of the Chicago Transit Authority).

A pre-dedication publicity photo taken at the Adams-Jackson station in the new State Street Subway on September 20, 1943 (Peter Fish Studios, Eric Bronsky Collection)

The South Shore Line, once a sister railroad to the North Shore Line, operates electric trains between Chicago and South Bend, Indiana. The old 1920's-era cars shown here were retired in 1983 and the Northern Indiana Commuter Transportation District presently operates the South Shore passenger service with newer cars. Today's Millennium Park was built directly above this area (Eric Bronsky photo).

following page
A train of wooden rapid transit cars (left) meets a Loop-bound North Shore train on Wells Street Bridge. The North Shore Line provided frequent service between downtown Chicago, downtown Milwaukee and several intermediate communities until 1963. In the background is the Merchandise Mart. Built by Marshall Field & Co. in 1930, it was then the largest building int the world (Eric Bronsky Collection).

The Prosperous Twenties

The decade of the twenties was a marvelous era for downtown. The city exuded an abundance of wealth and vigor. All of the State Street department stores were in their prime. Magnificent new beaux-arts skyscrapers with elegant spires soared above the dwindling number of post-fire loft buildings. The Balaban & Katz partners were building one ornate movie palace after another and the various visual and performing art venues were flourishing.

There were fine restaurants where workers and visitors could enjoy a sumptuous meal and visitors from out of town could stay at elegant new hotels like the Morrison, Bismarck, Sherman House, LaSalle, Blackstone, Stevens (now the Chicago Hilton and Towers), and Palmer House (now the Palmer House Hilton).

City planners implemented some key components of the Burnham Plan during this dynamic period. Replacement of the old Rush Street swing bridge with a new double-deck bascule bridge connecting Michigan Avenue to the city's North Side was completed in 1920. The area immediately surrounding the new bridge and its long approach ramps was extensively redeveloped. Together with a stunning ensemble of new office towers and a riverfront esplanade that was added later, the ornate bridge and widened thoroughfare served as a majestic new gateway between downtown and the North Side, beautifying the lakefront and improving travel.

In cooperation with the Lakefront Ordinance, which the City Council passed in 1919, the Illinois Central Railroad depressed their tracks below the grade of Michigan Avenue and electrified IC commuter trains. This long-sought improvement enhanced the desirability of South Michigan Boulevard and Grant Park.

Promoters advocated expansion of downtown southward along Michigan, Wabash, and State, but instead a northward migration began as soon as the new bridge was completed. This trend would culminate in a retail district that catered to the luxury trade, eventually surpassing State Street. South Michigan Boulevard was enriched by cultural institutions and grand hotels, but it never evolved into the fashionable retail destination that its planners originally envisioned.

Just west of Michigan, the old South Water Street Market had become a squalid and congested hurdle to north-south traffic, hampering improvements to the north boundary of downtown. As soon as this market could be relocated further west, bulldozers moved in and leveled the shabby buildings along the south bank of the river. South Water Street was then rebuilt into the much wider and two-level Wacker Drive that we know today. It was the first major downtown project designed to reduce traffic congestion by separating freight and service vehicles from pedestrians and auto traffic.

Along the river and its branches, modern bascule bridges gradually replaced the clumsy and antiquated swing bridges whose center piers obstructed navigation. The new bridges were more reliable and reduced dwell time for vehicular traffic.

Yet another obstacle that thwarted southward expansion of downtown was a kink in the South Branch of the Chicago River. A new riverbed was dug, and the old channel was filled in, thus freeing up land that would otherwise have no practical use. Unfortunately this massive public works project was completed just as the Depression was getting underway, so apart from some rerouted railroad tracks, the reclaimed land remained essentially undeveloped until the 1980s.

So vital did the Loop district become that everyday life in Chicago appeared to revolve around going downtown. Exponential growth of street traffic through downtown rendered ineffective the various improvements to street and transit infrastructure that were intended to alleviate congestion. Streetcars bunched up behind traffic and inched along, only to be further delayed by frequent bridge openings. Underground subways were proposed to siphon traffic from the Loop "L," which was operating beyond capacity.

Not every aspect of 1920s Chicago was positive. The Prohibition Act of 1919 helped to foment the rise of organized crime under Al Capone, a slick mob kingpin whose control extended to city legislators. Chicago already had a reputation for being a rough-and-tumble town, but the gunshots from the gangland violence reverberated around the world, casting a dark pall over the city that people still talked about decades later.

Michigan Boulevard, looking northerly from the steps of the
Art Institute at Adams in the mid-1920s. Originally published in the
Chicago Daily News on March 17, 1927,

This sequence of photos shows the Harris and Selwyn Theatres
under construction at the southwest corner of Dearborn and Lake.
The building was erected in a remarkably short time. In this
scene dated September 9, 1921, rubble from demolished buildings
on the site is still being removed (photographer unknown, courtesy
of the Chicago History Museum, ICHi-31420).

The steel framework for the upper levels was well underway by
early December. (photographer unknown, courtesy of the Chicago
History Museum, ICHi-31421).

By February of 1922, the exterior of the building was nearly completed
(Chicago Architectural Photographing Co., courtesy of the Chicago History
Museum, ICHi-31422)

The Donovan Affair was featured at the Selwyn in 1927. In later years the theatres
were renamed Michael Todd and Cinestage. Goodman Theatre, which occupies
this site today, built an entirely new facility behind the restored façade
(photographer unknown, courtesy of the Chicago History Museum, ICHi-31749).

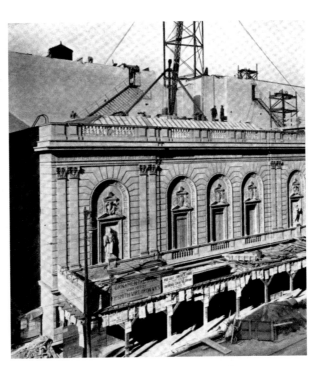

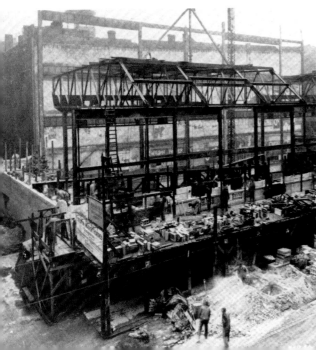

In 1923 the McVickers Theatre on Madison between State and Dearborn featured Agnes Ayres in Racing Hearts and the Theodore Roberts Symphony Orchestra (photographer unknown, courtesy of the Chicago History Museum, ICHi-36039)

Early view of the Woods Theatre at the northwest corner of Randolph and Dearborn, before construction of a more elaborate marquee (photographer unknown, courtesy of the Chicago History Museum, ICHi-19967).

The Sherman House hotel in 1929. Located at the northwest corner of Randolph and Clark, the James R. Thompson Center occupies its site today (Chicago Architectural Photographing Co., courtesy of the Chicago History Museum, ICHi-21026).

center left
The southwest corner of Franklin and South Water, just prior to construction of Wacker Drive (Eric Bronsky Collection).

top right
Adams Street looking east from Franklin. At right is the Marshall Field & Co. wholesale warehouse (courtesy of the Chicago Transit Authority).

center right
Clark Street looking south in front of City Hall (courtesy of the Chicago Transit Authority).

bottom right
LaSalle Street and the LaSalle Hotel, looking north from Madison. LaSalle Street Bridge is under construction in the background (courtesy of the Chicago Transit Authority).

next page
Michigan Avenue Bridge looking south towards Wacker Drive and the London Guarantee Building (courtesy of the Chicago Transit Authority).

R.T. 36
8-10

Two 1920 views of Michigan Avenue, one looking north from Randolph and the other from East South Water Street, show the improved roadway and approach to the new bridge (Eric Bronsky Collection).

Newly completed Wacker Drive between Franklin and Lake in 1926
(Kaufman & Fabry photo).

Michigan Boulevard looking southwesterly from Grant Park
(Kaufman & Fabry photo).

Wacker Drive looking east towards State Street (courtesy of the Chicago Transit Authority).

Wacker Drive looking west towards Wabash (courtesy of the Chicago Transit Authority).

Straightening the South Branch of the Chicago River in 1929 (Chicago Aerial Survey Co. photo, Eric Bronsky Collection).

The Civic Opera House under construction in 1929 (Kaufman & Fabry photo, courtesy of the Chicago History Museum, ICHi-31434).

The lobby staircase of the Civic Opera House (Chicago Architectural Photographing Co., courtesy of the Chicago History Museum, ICHi-20884).

following page
Michigan Boulevard and Grant Park looking north from Monroe (Chicago Architectural Photographing Co., courtesy of the Chicago Transit Authority).

Myles Jarrow

I remember going downtown with my mother when I was four years old, particularly on the Illinois Central Suburban trains before they were electrified in 1926. Downtown held great fascination for me: Lots of people, the tall buildings, and especially the wide variety of streetcars.

I remember the first time that I was in a movie theatre— I was only 3 1/2 or 4 years old. I didn't like the darkness, and I was very unhappy! But I got over that rather quickly. Seeing those Balaban & Katz movie palaces—and I use the word palaces advisedly as opposed to *theatres*—I thought that all movie theatres would be like these. But as I began to travel and see theatres in other cities, I found that Chicago's theatres were decidedly above the rest.

I also remember the stage performances at the Palace and Chicago Theatres, and I recollect that there was very good talent, at least for those times. I wonder if what I thought was good talent back then would go over well nowadays.

My parents also took my brother and me to museums, particularly the Field Museum of Natural History and the Shedd Aquarium. The Art Institute came somewhat later, and perhaps in those days I really didn't appreciate art like I learned to appreciate it as an adult. I also visited Navy Pier, but I'll admit: Rather than be interested in the ships that came in, I was much more interested in watching the Grand Avenue streetcar as it came out on the Pier!

My father's company manufactured refrigerator door gaskets. He started the business, called Jarrow Products, in 1927 and it was located at what is now 420 N. LaSalle Street. I began working summers there in 1936 or 1937. It was at the north end of the LaSalle Street streetcar tunnel under the Chicago River. In the days before air conditioning, it was great during a summer day to board the streetcar at the corner of LaSalle and Hubbard and ride through the underwater tunnel. It was so nice and cool under the river, but then we came back to reality when the car came out of the tunnel at Randolph Street.

LaSalle Street looking north from Washington. In the distance a streetcar is emerging from the tunnel beneath the Chicago River (Chicago Architectural Photographing Co., Eric Bronsky Collection)

The Chicago Theatre in 1927 (Kaufman & Fabry photo, courtesy of the Chicago History Museum, ICHi-10987).

Josephine Baskin Minow

Before I was born, my father had an advertising firm called Carson-Baskin Advertising Agency, where they created ads for Richman Brothers, Maurice L. Rothschild, and The Hub, aka Henry C. Lytton and Company. He also handled advertising for Hart, Schaffner and Marx. All of those stores were located on State Street.

One day the Hart people came to see dad, telling him they wanted to open a retail outlet for their men's clothing. But they did not want to use their name. It was the mid-to-late '20s, and their suggestion was twofold: could they call it the Baskin Store, and would dad become president and general manager of the State Street store? (Eventually there were five or six stores). Dad left the agency, managed the new store, and became involved with the State Street Council for several years.

He was an extraordinary man. Born and raised in Chicago, one of seven children of Russian immigrant parents, he ended his formal education at eighth grade. Yet he went on to lecture at the University of Chicago. A voracious reader, he was a knowledgeable collector of rare first editions and a charter member of the first Great Books course initiated by Mortimer Adler and Robert Maynard Hutchins. He was, indeed, a self-educated man.

After he left the Baskin stores, he opened an advertising agency called the Salem N. (N for nothing) Baskin Advertising Agency, which also handled public relations for such places as Goldblatt Stores where he kept a little office for himself on State Street.

A Baskin store at the southeast corner of Washington and Clark
(courtesy of the Chicago Transit Authority).

following page
State Street looking north from Van Buren in 1924
(Eric Bronsky Collection).

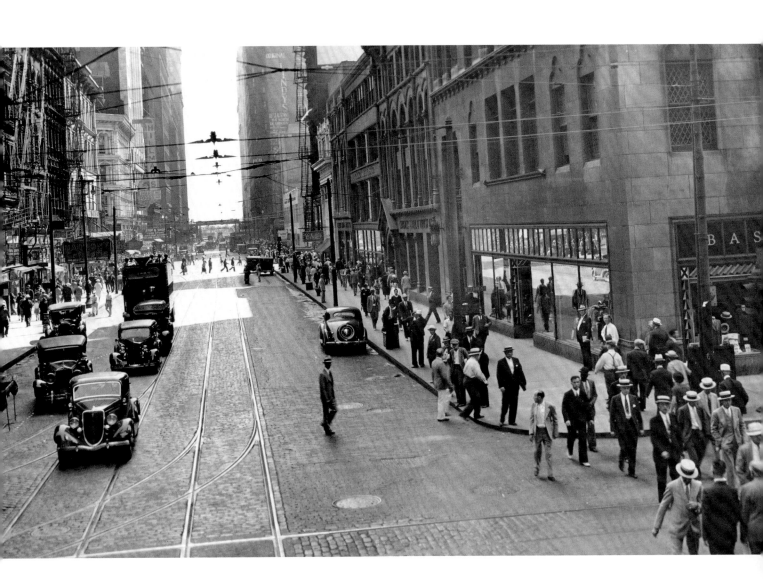

PART II
TWO CHALLENGING DECADES
1930s & 1940s

Chicago has slogged through turbulent events ranging from fires, wars, and riots to local corruption and organized crime with remarkable resiliency. But with the onset of the Great Depression, unemployment and homelessness overtook prosperity. As elsewhere in the United States, the economic catastrophe had a significant impact on Chicago and recovery was painstakingly slow.

Manufacturing bore the brunt of the slowdown. Factories laid off tens of thousands of workers, affecting much of Chicago's working and lower middle class population. For recently arrived European immigrants with their sturdy resolve and strong work ethics, not being able to find a job was unimaginable. Some people had the fortitude to become peddlers; they combed streets and alleys looking for discarded items to resell, sharpened knives, or sold home-grown fruits, vegetables, and hand-made goods on downtown streets. Regardless, life marched relentlessly onward because everyday needs had to be met.

Downtown did not, however, become a ghost town. Scores of smaller downtown businesses closed, but most of the larger ones remained open, though in some cases dangling precariously from shoestring budgets. Store merchandise shifted from luxury towards necessity. Some loft buildings on the outer fringes of the Loop became flophouses whose residents took their meals at makeshift soup kitchens or "beaneries" where a bowl of baked beans cost a few pennies.

Not all businesses and individuals were adversely affected. That dreadful axiom, "the rich get richer, and the poor get poorer," was partly true. Walgreen's, Woolworth's, and Kresge's were among the thriving State Street retailers during this period. These stores fared well by featuring low cost quality products and were able to continue employing many workers. Their inexpensive lunch counters and soda fountains would remain popular for many decades following the Depression.

Remarkably, two new flagship department stores debuted on State Street during this sluggish period. Sears, Roebuck & Co. took over the former Siegel Cooper & Co. building in 1932, and Goldblatt's bought out the Davis Store in 1936.

Buildings under construction before the crash were duly completed and occupied, but after the splendid Field Building (also known as the LaSalle Bank Building) was topped off in 1934, it would be two long decades before any further skyscraper projects were begun in the Loop area.

The municipal government was beleaguered by the mounting fiscal crisis and angry disputes rising from the growth of organized labor. In 1931, voters seeking reform unseated incumbent Republican Mayor William "Big Bill" Thompson and over time became increasingly loyal to the Democratic Party. Subsequent civic leaders were expected to do more for the poor and the working class. Thus the Democratic "machine" was born. The city's problems could not be solved overnight, but each successive administration did progressively more to get the city back on track and plan for the future.

Just when the sense of hopelessness and despair seemed to reach a nadir, the opening of the Century of Progress Exposition in 1933 stimulated economic recovery by bolstering hope and optimism for the future. Apart from beautification of the lakefront, a residual benefit of this two-year event was the introduction of streamlining, a modernist art form that branched out from the popular Art Deco movement. First popularized by the Budd Company's design for a railroad passenger train prominently displayed at the Fair during 1934, it expanded boldly into architecture, the visual arts, and even consumer products such as toasters and vacuum cleaners.

Also during 1933, Prohibition was repealed as part of the nation's comprehensive effort towards stimulating business and discouraging organized crime.

In the mid-30s, the federal government established the Work Projects Administration (WPA) along with other relief programs to provide employment and aid. Federal funds put many unemployed Chicagoans back to work on long-planned projects to relieve downtown's traffic congestion. Lake Shore Drive and the State Street subway were built during this period, and planning of the area's first superhighways began in earnest.

Ironically, it took a crisis of an entirely different nature to end the Depression. As the country geared up for World War II and shipped masses of enlisted men overseas, factories had fewer workers available to fill the rapidly multiplying production orders, so they hired and trained women, elderly, and physically disabled people to operate the assembly lines. The lure of such jobs attracted people from other parts of the country to Chicago, notably African-Americans from areas rife with unemployment and racial segregation.

Downtown Chicago's role as the nation's transportation hub became critical during the war years. Some of the largest and most important military training facilities in the country were located in the north suburbs, and military personnel from all over the country traveled to and from Chicago by train. The Municipal Pier (Navy Pier) and several downtown buildings were pressed into service as military facilities. USO and Chicago Servicemen's Centers served thousands of men daily.

Gasoline rationing, in combination with heightened demand for local and intercity travel, strained Chicago's transportation infrastructure beyond its limits. Ridership on streetcar, elevated, interurban, and intercity rail lines reached all-time highs. There was a moratorium on most building projects because construction materials were needed for the war effort, but work on the State Street Subway was prioritized. Its completion in 1943 relieved some but not all of the congestion on the Loop "L."

During such difficult times, Chicagoans sought diversions more than ever in the form of recreation and entertainment. Parks and neighborhood venues were convenient, but downtown was really the place to be! The movie palaces had elaborate stage shows, and large restaurants and nightclubs featured top popular music artists of the era along with variety and comedy acts.

Following the nationwide victory celebrations in the summer of 1945, the return to normalcy was incremental and not without hurdles. Much of the public works infrastructure had been neglected since the onset of the Depression. Public transit was outmoded and deteriorating—indeed, the private companies that owned and operated the various modes of service had been in bankruptcy since the Depression. With growing competition from automobiles, there was clearly no chance for their recovery. To prevent the collapse of this essential public utility and institute a program of capital improvements, the city established the Chicago Transit Authority in 1947 to purchase, consolidate, and operate the street railway, bus, and elevated lines under one municipal umbrella.

State Street looking north at Randolph during a State Street Council promotion in June 1933 (Webster Bros. photo).

Adams Street looking east towards Dearborn. The familiar Berghoff Restaurant sign is visible in the background (courtesy of the Chicago Transit Authority).

Celebrants ride one of ten special trains to the dedication
ceremony of the brand new State Street Subway on October 16, 1943
(courtesy of the Chicago Transit Authority).

Two Carson Pirie Scott & Co. store window displays during
World War II (Chicago Public Library, Special Collections and
Preservation Division).

Myles Jarrow

I would hear about the Depression from my schoolteachers, but I never saw any evidence of it in my own home. If there were hard times within our family, it was never mentioned around the dining room table. Dad didn't seem to be nervous at all, and everything seemed to be going in a positive direction.

On the other hand, in school, many of the teachers would speak about what was happening during the Depression. At that time, the schoolteachers in the Chicago Public School system had not been paid for at least two years, maybe longer. Finally, in 1934, they received their back pay and then their regular pay resumed. Needless to say, the teachers were extremely happy and many of them then had money to take a trip since all of their expenses had previously been covered through savings, family, etc.

Downtown didn't seem particularly different during the Depression years. It was still lively with a lot of people and traffic. I do recall a nice looking man in a blue suit on roller skates with sandwich board signs on his front and back saying, "I want a job!" and indicating his qualifications. I've often wondered what happened to him.

The World's Fair was a wonderful boon for the public; it gave people something else to think about besides the Depression itself. I recall the adult entrance fee into the World's Fair was 50 cents. Today it would probably be $20-$25 for the same type of exposition.

I would describe downtown as becoming contemporary—there was quite a trend towards modernization in those years. By the forties I was much more interested in what was around me than I had been in my earlier years. Upon graduating from the University of Chicago in June of 1942, I took a full-time job with *Mass Transportation* Magazine. It was published at 431 S. Dearborn Street, and I stayed with them until I was inducted into the army in January 1943.

During the war, Chicago had a reputation for being very hospitable to servicemen. There were several USO service clubs, which were wonderful places for servicemen to go to enjoy a respite. A man in uniform could ride a streetcar or bus free of charge. Servicemen were able to get tickets to legitimate plays at greatly reduced prices, whereas prior to World War II I remember hearing stories about Chicagoans receiving less than a warm welcome while visiting other cities.

I remember in particular a story told by a girl in grammar school. Her mother went into a beauty shop in some resort area and happened to say she was from Chicago. The woman sitting in the chair next to her said, "You're from Chicago? I don't want to be next to you!" and immediately left! Yes, Chicago once had that kind of reputation! But all of that gradually changed.

I did not go back to work for my dad's company immediately after the war. I had always wanted to be in the transportation business, so my friend Frank Butts and I went into the bus business in Lincoln, Illinois, where we operated a fleet of four transit buses. But by 1948 I began to see the handwriting on the wall. I had anticipated that people would continue to be enthusiastic users of public transit after the war, but that turned out to be a pipe dream. As more people bought automobiles, fewer would ride our buses, so I saw no future for myself in that business.

Well, I sold the operation in 1948, came back home, and went into the family business, which pleased my father tremendously. In those years I would go downtown frequently. I would meet friends there for lunch, and on weekends we would go to a movie. My brother and I continued on with the family business until I retired in 1992. A high-rise now occupies the block where the business had been.

Kay Mayer

I grew up in Chicago on the South Side in Kenwood at 4753 Kimbark Avenue. My earliest memories about downtown Chicago focused on the store windows, especially Marshall Field's, during Christmas time. The displays were always mechanized, not just plain windows. I remember seeing Santa Claus at the store, and there was always a line of kids waiting to see him. The Walnut Room was one of my favorite places. Downstairs in the basement they had a cafeteria, and there was a waiting room on the third floor. They sold Frango mint candy on the first floor, and there was a food store on the seventh floor.

I also remember Mandel Brothers, the Fair, the Boston Store, and Carson's, and there was a famous candy store called Kranz's on State Street. I went to the Chicago Theatre, but also to Balaban and Katz's Tivoli Theatre on the South Side. I used to go the theatres, such as the Schubert, the Selwyn, and the Harris, which later became the Goodman Theatre. We also went to the Woods confectionary stores, with one on Monroe Street and one on North Michigan Avenue, where they had marvelous candy and wonderful sodas and sundaes. My father was in the candy business and had a company called Peerless that made hard candies.

When we went downtown, it was with my father's car, rather than by bus. He would drive us, and we would see the windows at Christmas time at Field's and Carson's. As a matter of fact, my husband's family, the Mayers, owned the store that preceded Carson Pirie Scott. It was called Schlesinger and Mayer, and they were at State and Madison.

The store was built by Adler and Sullivan. In fact Dankmar Adler was my great uncle by marriage. Adler also built the Auditorium Building, and he was an engineer as well as an architect. The Auditorium had a restaurant in addition to a hotel and the theatre, the place where Roosevelt University was later located. My father-in-law founded the Mayer, Meyer, Austrian and Platt law firm, one of the largest firms.

The Blackhawk was one of my favorite restaurants downtown. I remember the Garrick, Oriental, Palace, State-Lake, and Chicago Theatres. Then, there were Hillmans, Stop and Shop, and Gapers for food. At the famous Henrici's Restaurant, their motto was "no orchestral din." Maillard's Restaurant was on Jackson and Michigan and was an excellent restaurant. On the top of the Sherman House was the Bal Tabarin, a nightclub. Then, there was the Old Heidelberg and Trader Vic's.

Randolph Street looking east from LaSalle (courtesy of the Chicago Transit Authority).

following page
Looking east on Randolph Street from Clark in 1931 (courtesy of the Chicago Transit Authority).

GARRICK THEATRE
ORIENTAL
GARRICK
RESTAURANT
WE SERVE GOOD FOOD

Josephine Baskin Minow

I have lived here since my birth in 1926, and I continue to be filled with awe and wonder at all Chicago has to offer, as the city continues to grow and glow and give. Chicago has a heart; a big heart. Twice we moved away from Chicago to Washington, D.C.: once in the early '50s, and again in the early '60s. And twice everyone said, "You'll never come home again," and twice I said, "Just you wait and see!"

I grew up at 429 Briar Place, just south of Belmont Avenue on the North Side. Our second floor apartment, where we lived for 20 years, was just steps away from Sheridan Road. Because my parents didn't drive, we had no car and thought nothing of walking everywhere, or taking the bus or streetcar. Nettlehorst Elementary School was only three blocks away, and later, when I went to Senn High School, I climbed aboard the streetcar at Broadway and Belmont and then walked five minutes to school from the car stop. No big deal.

As soon as I was old enough, I would often ride the bus downtown after school to visit Marshall Field and Company. Then I would wander around the Loop, dipping into Mandel Brothers and Carson Pirie Scott and sometimes stopping for a soda or some coffee candy at the famous Kranz's. In those long ago days, parents had no need to worry about allowing their children to travel around the city alone, and the Loop was a treasure trove of surprises and secrets for me.

In the '30s and '40s, Field's had an antique silver department, an antique furniture department, and an antique jewelry department, plus a section for paintings, one for stamps and one for rare books. There was also a playroom for kids and a gigantic toy department on the fourth floor. On the third floor, I would get lost in the book section where I could sit on the floor and read to my heart's delight for hours. Bliss!

I didn't have the money to shop, so I was satisfied just looking around. But one day, I spied a pair of pink satin pajamas with navy blue trim at Carson's. They were on sale, and I just had to have them. So, I carefully selected a pair my

size and then charged them to my parents' account, but not before taking advantage of having them monogrammed for free making them non-returnable. It was that "for free" that got me. Talk about chutzpah. I was twelve years old.

I remember going to the Chicago Theatre from time to time to see the latest movie and the bonus, a glorious live stage show. Another drawing card in the Loop was the Empire Room at the Palmer House where leading performers of stage, screen, and radio made appearances. I will never forget being t-h-i-s close to Jack Benny and watching the Merriel Abbott Dancers was always a delight, especially since some of my schoolmates were taking classes with her and perhaps hoped that one day they might appear on the Empire Room stage.

The ground floor of the Palmer House, just like today, housed various shops. The one that took my breath away was the magic store. Once inside, you could watch wondrous magic tricks being performed. And though we pleaded and pleaded, the secret of the trick could not be revealed until you bought it. Talk about come-ons!

I loved going to Henrici's Restaurant on West Randolph Street with my family. It was an elegant landmark, and it was always very festive. And of course there was Old Heidelberg across the street, as I recall. One night, we were celebrating my parents' 25th anniversary with my sister, brother, and Uncle Neel at that restaurant. It was quite a large and fancy establishment, with elegant tables on a main floor and up on a balcony. Waiting for our food to arrive, we were getting

restless and my dad suggested we dip our fingers in our water glasses and run them around the rims. He was always full of fun. But this time we created quite a stir.

We were positioned on the balcony a fair distance from the orchestra where, unbeknownst to us, a broadcast was being routed over AM radio – "Music from Old Heidelberg." The tones we had produced entertained us so completely we didn't notice the waiters and radio engineer trying to track down the source of the unholy din that was going out over the air waves. That is, until from three sides they converged upon the source of the noise and demanded that we stop gumming up their broadcast. We did!

One summer when I was in college, I worked for my father, Salem N. Baskin, at his advertising agency in the 333 North Michigan Avenue building. I remember a day in July when a summer storm hit the city—fierce winds and heavy downpour. Dad took his usual bus home from the work and walked the short distance from the bus to our apartment.

Just as he reached the door of our building, dripping wet from the rain, a Yellow cab drove up and I got out of it, untouched by rain and wind. I waltzed to greet him. Stunned, he managed to get out, "How can you afford to take a taxicab?" Without dripping a syllable, I shot back,

"You could too, if you had a rich father!" He dined out on that story for years.

When I graduated from Northwestern University in 1948, I was fortunate enough to fulfill my dream of getting a job on State Street in merchandising and advertising. I was accepted into an executive training program at Mandel Brothers. I had wanted to go into a similar program at Field's, the tonier store down the block, but I was not accepted. After barely a week in the program at Mandel's, however, a call came from Field's asking me to come into its training program. I was tempted and really wanted to, but I had made a commitment to Mandel Brothers and felt I had to keep it.

Soon after the Mandel's program was finished, I was assigned to become assistant to the director of advertising, Esther Friedman, who taught me even more than I had learned in the store's classes. We became good friends until her death many years later.

The Loop was a great venue for what we called legitimate theatre. I would go with friends or family to the Great Northern, the Erlanger, the Harris, and Selwyn. Of course, we went to the first run movie houses, such as the Palace, the State-Lake, and the Oriental, in addition to the wondrous Chicago Theatre.

previous page
Henrici's Restaurant and Hoe Sai Gai, a popular Chinese eatery,
stood on the south side of Randolph Street between Dearborn and Clark
(courtesy of the Chicago History Museum, ICHi-27893).

This image was the product of a 1936 campaign by the State Street
Council to promote holiday shopping (Chicago Public Library, Special
Collections and Preservation Division).

Mandel Brothers' main department store building at the northeast
corner of State and Madison was completed in 1912 (courtesy of the
Chicago History Museum, ICHi-17546).

Bernard Judge

I was born in 1940 and raised on Chicago's South Side, first on Ingleside Avenue in Holy Cross Parish. Then, in 1944, we moved to 79th and Euclid, a block from Jeffrey Boulevard, and lived in a little bungalow that still stands there. The neighborhood was either South Shore or South Chicago because 79th Street was the dividing line, but, for me it was the parish, Our Lady of Peace. Later, when people would talk about South Shore, I would say, "No, it was either Lady of Peace or St. Philip Neri or St. Brides." The steel plants were a mile and a half east of us, and you could see the smoke coming from the stacks of the mills. If the smoke was pouring out, that meant work for men. No smoke, no work.

In order for us to get downtown, we could take the Illinois Central ("IC") at 71st Street or ride a bus to 63rd Street and Stony Island, the end of the line for the CTA Howard-Jackson Park line. We would get on the "L" there and take it downtown. If we were flush with cash, we would take the IC, but you couldn't get transfers if you took the IC and your ride ended at Randolph Street. Then you would have to walk. So, if we were going to move around the city a lot, we would take the bus to the "L" at 63rd and Stony Island and then go downtown. The station was located in the Woodlawn neighborhood, and it could be a bit "tricky" at times for us because we were in "enemy territory." The guys in that neighborhood weren't our friends, and we weren't their friends. By the time I was in high school, the community around 63rd and Stony Island had already changed and was primarily African-American. It took years for me to overcome the racist world of my childhood. Fortunately for me, my parents—my father in particular—would not allow talk of prejudice in our home.

Downtown was an exciting place to go, and the first time we went there was in the 1940s after WWII for the parade that came right down Michigan Avenue, including Sherman tanks and General Douglas MacArthur. It was in the summertime, and the tanks were so heavy that they just tore up the asphalt. I was five years old at that time, and Michigan Avenue, on the west side of the avenue from the river to Adams, with few exceptions, has changed very little from those years. That was my first memory of being downtown.

I started high school at Leo on 79th Street, three blocks west of Halsted. I totally knew the boundaries of my neighborhood and my parish in terms of where it was safe to go and where it might not be. Around us, the neighborhoods and parishes were primarily Irish, although there were also Italians and Germans and Eastern Europeans and Mexicans and blacks. The growth of the African American community near us came much later in the 1960s, and when I got out of military service, the neighborhood was beginning to change from white to black, and block busting was a common tactic in those years to scare whites to move out of the area.

When we took the "L" downtown, we would get off at Washington and right upstairs was Marshall Field's and State Street. To me, the State Street area was an exotic and wonderful place filled with all kinds of amazing things to see and do. That ranged from the movie theatres such as the Chicago Theatre and the State-Lake Theatre to the McVickers, Oriental, Clark, and Loop Theatres. There was an arcade on Randolph, west of State, on the south side of the street, where you could go and play amusement games. I remember that Pixley & Ehlers had great sweet rolls, and we loved going there. On those infrequent occasions when we were downtown, we might go to the Chicago Theatre to see a movie and a stage show, such as one I saw starring Spike Jones. Another time, we saw a stage show in between a double-feature. The show starred Denise Darcel, a French singer, who was a bit zaftig with a sweet voice.

While downtown, we would roam around Field's and try on clothes but never buy them. One of the games we played at Field's was to get from the bottom of the store to the top by

going up the down escalators. Once in a while, the store guards would get angry and chase us out of the store. Although there were magnificent places in the store, like the Walnut Room, they were completely out of our financial reach. I remember Uncle Mistletoe and the Christmas tree and all the wonderful stuff that was there.

However, in those growing up years, we usually stayed in our neighborhood and did not go downtown that often. I had a friend who said his world began at 71st Street and ended at 83rd Street, between Stony Island and Lake Michigan, and that he never wanted to be anywhere else. He determined that you went downtown to get your marriage certificate and little else. Simply put, going downtown was for special occasions and it was a little bit exotic to be there. Of course, we grew up near the Avalon Theatre on 79th Street which was a fantastic theatre, and it was beautiful like the Southtown Theatre.

As for the few major events our family celebrated, we went to Henrici's on Randolph, and I remember the white tablecloths and crystal as well as the fact that Henrici's was at the top of our "restaurant food chain." It was way upscale, just like Shangri-La and Fritzels, and, for me, it was a marvelous place. I also remember that the Blackhawk Restaurant on Wabash was well known for its steaks and prime rib and the famous spinning salad bowl. Trader Vic's, located in the Palmer House was also very popular, as was the wonderful Well of the Sea in the Sherman House.

Chicago's downtown was also a great, great place to hear jazz, something that was important to me as I grew up. In fact, I started going to the Blue Note when I was in my teens, and they had a section where teenagers could listen to the jazz even though they couldn't be served liquor. The club was located upstairs in a building on Clark and Madison, across from what is now Chase Bank. I remember when The Modern Jazz Quartet was the fill-in band during intermission, and they were one of the greatest groups I ever heard. There were jazz bars all over downtown and the Near North Side, including Mister Kelly's on Rush Street and the London House at the London Guarantee Building at Michigan and Wacker. Both places were owned and operated by the Marienthal Brothers, who were able to discover young, talented musicians and comedians, and then sign them to long term contracts. Those performers knew that if they could play at Mister Kelly's and the London House, their careers would take off...and they did, including such stars as Nancy Wilson, Sarah Vaughn, Ramsey Lewis, Shelley Berman, and Mort Sahl.

In high school, if we went downtown with our dates, we might go to the observation deck at the Prudential Building, known as the "Top of the Rock." In the '50s, the Italian Village was the restaurant to go to after high school proms, and that was the night when you dressed up in your white tuxedo with a cummerbund. The main library was a part of my life downtown, and when I got into high school and transferred to Fenwick High School from the South Side to Oak Park, I went to the main public library on Randolph and the Newberry Library on Clark Street. High school for me was a very tough academic environment, and you often used the resources of those libraries. The library was a magnificent building, and still is.

Charles de Gaulle cavalcade in 1945, looking south on State from Madison
(Chicago Public Library, Special Collections and Preservation Division).

George E. Kanary

I was born in the Oakland neighborhood on Chicago's South Side, but my earliest memories are of when we lived in Bridgeport. I've got all the pleasant memories that any kid would have, growing up in what I assumed was the best neighborhood in the world. The aroma from the stockyards used to pervade the neighborhood but most of the residents took little notice of it at all.

It was so different then. People would dress properly to go downtown, even just for the mundane task of shopping. My mother and I would meet my father for lunch, often under the Marshall Field's clock, once or twice a week. His law firm was in the former Conway building at the southwest corner of Clark and Washington, directly across from the County Building. Today this beautifully restored building is known as Burnham Center. We would go to a restaurant or possibly to the Ontra Cafeteria on Wabash, or to the wonderful burger restaurant named O'Connell's. They had four places in Chicago, and there was one kitty-corner from his office; it was done in a half-timbered style.

As a youngster, your interests are kind of limited, but I remember being impressed with the Michigan Avenue skyline. When my mother took me to a department store, we would go to the toy department and sometimes I'd be allowed to make a selection. Incidentally, the Fair Store had the finest toy department in all Chicago, bar none! It occupied a big space on the eighth floor and blew Marshall Field's right out of the water! However, it was only open from Thanksgiving to Christmas Eve, and then the toy department reverted to a much smaller space on the seventh floor.

The selection of toys during the war years was pretty much limited to those made of wood or cardboard, with all metal going for the war effort. Still, with this limitation, it was a wonderland for me because they also had two amusement park style trains that you could ride! The trains departed and returned to a wrought iron station structure and raced along behind walls and partitions in a secret world that only kids could go to, looping around the enormous electric train display at the outer end before heading back. It was electric powered, of course. Then we would often go to the wonderful cafeteria on the seventh floor. Their macaroni and cheese was every kid's favorite, as good as it gets.

My mother didn't go through Sears or Goldblatt's. She didn't have anything in particular against these stores; it's just that most of her shopping was confined to the north end, to Carson's, Mandel Brothers, and The Boston Store. Even though The Fair Store was towards the south end, she really liked that store and so did I.

The Boston Store had a fascinating Wimpy's restaurant inside the store. It might have been on the same floor as the toy department but it was in their traditional cottage style, a building built right within the store. They also had a barbershop with those kid-size chairs that I haven't seen in years; they're always pale green porcelain.

What a great time to be a kid, and how sorry I feel for those today who know only the barren confines of a Toys "R" Us store or a Wal-Mart.

My father gave up his car – he had a 1931 Studebaker President which he gave to a nephew of his in 1937– so I never saw the car and my father died in 1947. So we went everywhere by streetcar or taxicab, and somehow I became a streetcar fan. A good bit of the time shopping with my mother was spent breaking away and looking out from a department store window where you could watch the streetcars on State Street. My mother, who was not a native Chicagoan, seemed to know Chicago like the back of her hand. When we would go downtown or visit my grandmother on the North Side, we would take a different route each time. Streetcars did carry some big loads during the war years.

When my father's health failed, I was sent to a military school in LaGrange, Illinois, but I usually came home on weekends. My mother and I often went somewhere nice downtown for dinner on Sunday. Then I would leave her and head for Union Station to ride the Burlington back to school. But many times I would stand at the south end of the platforms for several hours watching the great Limited trains,

State Street looking north from Madison in 1935 (courtesy of the Chicago Transit Authority).

The New York Central Railroad's premier passenger train, the brand new
streamlined 20th Century Limited, is seen here departing Chicago on
June 15 1938 (Alexander Maxwell photo, Kalmbach Publishing Co. collection).

The Fair Store at the northwest corner of State and Adams in 1930.
Originally published in the *Chicago Daily News;* photographer unknown
(Copyright by Chicago Sun-Times, Inc. Reprinted with permission).

A Chicago Surface Lines bus and streetcar southbound at State and Adams
in October 1946, prior to the CTA era (courtesy of the Chicago Transit Authority).

many still powered by steam locomotives, depart for all points of the compass. Some of my schoolmates knew where to find me and occasionally we would get back late, having to face the wrath of God for being AWOL.

After the loss of my dad, we moved to the Northwest Side, where my mother bought a rundown deli and completely overhauled it, making it into a popular neighborhood shopping spot. The area was not really a melting pot but was divided between Roman Catholic Polish, and Polish and Russian Jews. A large synagogue was almost directly across the street from her store, and I recall them asking me to go in there on Fridays to turn on the electric lights. I used to go to the Deborah Jewish Boys Club, my buddies passing me off as a blue-eyed, blond Jewish kid in order to use their well-equipped workshop.

Because my mother at first operated the store by herself with only me to help her when I was home from school, she could not leave, and so it became my responsibility to shop for her, go downtown to pay her mortgage, things like that. I would often walk out with up to $200 in my pocket—this was in 1947, when I was not yet ten years old! Many offices and businesses were still open half a day on Saturday, so if I got home quickly on a Saturday morning, I could still get back downtown to accomplish these chores, usually taking the Logan Square 'L' from the Division stop.

My mother loved to entertain at home or out, and occasionally, she would bring a friend or two along for Sunday dinner at the Stevens Hotel (now Hilton) Boulevard Room, which had the Ice Show to watch as you dined, or to Fritzel's. I clearly remember Mrs. Cook badgering me to get an autograph from Julius La Rosa, who would dine at Fritzel's when he was performing at the Chicago Theatre. Many times we went to Drake's, which later became Mayor's Row. Sometimes there was time to catch a movie after dinner.

I loved the Ontra Cafeteria on Wabash. The Ontra had a toy box from which a youngster could make a selection, assuming he or she had finished everything on their plate. The toys or prizes were on the order of those found in Cracker Jack boxes. Sometimes we would go to DeMet's, a place which I later learned was a comfortable environment for women to go alone. All of these places were locally owned and served good quality food at reasonable prices.

Henrici's was also a favorite from the time I was a very young kid. Their bakery in the front of the restaurant was spectacular also, and I was always fascinated by the big machine that wrapped the string around your purchases, although I guess other bakeries had them, too.

Across the street from Marshall Field's was Kranz's Candy Store, probably the finest confectionary this side of Vienna, Austria with its beautiful tall, curved glass windows facing State Street. It was a special treat.

Stop & Shop had a variety of merchandise that you would almost never see anywhere else. You would never find maple sugar, for example, and certainly not Bon Voyage baskets at the local grocery store or the A&P. During the war, when fresh meat was hard to come by, they always seemed to have a good selection. Of course you needed the proper ration points to buy any of it. I also remember walking down the aisles and noticing that they had canned rattlesnake. Also shad roe, which was a favorite of mine growing up and was far more common then. Watching the rapid skill of the package wrappers at Stop & Shop was fascinating, also classy—everything was wrapped in dark green paper and went into green shopping bags that had a carrying handle.

The space later occupied by Baer's Treasure Chest on Randolph Street was originally an upscale cocktail lounge named, I think, the Preview. This was directly across the street from the famous Old Heidelberg restaurant. Before Randolph was made one-way west, the Gray Line sightseeing bus used to park there facing east. Their sandwich board sign pointed out the wonderful sights that would be seen, including the 'Ghetto Market' (Maxwell Street) and the Stock Yards. The Stock Yards was the destination for many visitors to the city—they must have been impressed by Carl Sandburg's poetry.

As for the rest of the streets, I was fascinated by Clark Street because of the used bookstores in later years. You could spend the entire afternoon in one bookstore, come out with $2 worth of merchandise, and it would be a bag full of books. But I was always fascinated by the architecture along Dearborn Street, the elevated encircling everything, the streetcars running under the elevated, and the lineup of Chicago Motor Coach buses including double-deckers along State Street ready to head north from downtown. All of this was pretty overwhelming to a kid.

Jerry Field

In the late '40s, I was living in Albany Park and going to Roosevelt High School. On my 16th birthday, I was hired as an usher with Balaban and Katz Theatres. I got the job because I was able to change my high school class schedule so that I was through by 12:30 P.M. and could work from 2 to 10 P.M. Since I was available to work a full schedule, I was assigned to the Roosevelt Theatre in downtown Chicago. I would hop on the Ravenswood "L" at 12:30 P.M. and could arrive at the Roosevelt by 12:50 P.M., work as an usher, and still do my high school homework.

One day, the manager, Henry Potter, came in and said to me, "I don't want to disturb your homework, but John Balaban needs you to run some errands." Thus, I began to do errands for Mr. Balaban. When he found out that I was doing homework from 1 to 2 P.M., he would not allow me to come to the office before 2:15 P.M. I would work all afternoon running errands or just sit in his office with him.

When I graduated from Roosevelt High School, I decided to attend Wright Junior College. However, I didn't graduate from Wright before I went into the Army. When I completed my military service, I immediately went back to Balaban and Katz. In fact, I was still in my uniform and hadn't even been home yet when I got into town. Mr. Balaban said, "Well, you get your job back, but now I can't make you chief of service or in charge of anything. Instead, I'm going to make you an assistant manager at the State-Lake Theatre." At that point, I knew all the procedures, but Mr. Balaban said to me, "By the way, you can't get your job unless you go back to college. You are my employee and you are my friend, and you are going back to school."

So, I went over to Roosevelt University and showed them my GI Discharge. Since the university needed money and I had cash from the GI Bill, I was enrolled on the spot. They gave me credit for my work in the Army, and I graduated from Roosevelt in a year and a half, receiving a B.S. in Business Administration. The same day I was admitted to Roosevelt, I went back to Mr. Balaban and showed him that I had enrolled

in school. He asked, "Do you want to start work tonight?" I said, "These are the only clothes that I have." So, he said, "Well, we can take care of that. Can you still fit in your clothes that you wore before?" I said, "I doubt it." I went into the Army weighing 127 pounds, and I came out weighing 35 pounds more. He issued a voucher for me to buy a suit, and that was my homecoming present. Two days later I was at the State-Lake Theatre in the evening as assistant manager, working with the manager, a young man named Harry Odenthal, whose wife worked as a cashier at the Chicago Theatre located across State Street.

I worked there three nights a week, and in addition, I went to work as a copy boy at the *Chicago Sun-Times* on weekends because I needed the money. I was on the overnight shift from midnight to 8 A.M. I worked for Mr. Walsh, and one day, he called me into his office and said, "I understand that you have been nice enough to work an extra hour on Saturday until 9 P.M. and that you have been working with Kup." At that time, Irv Kupcinet's deadline was 8:40 A.M. on Saturday. He would walk in about 8 A.M., give me a list of calls to make, and I would just wake up people and check items for "Kup's Column." After two weeks, Mr. Walsh said to me, "How do you like working for Kup?" I said, "It's just fine." He asked, "Are you sure that everything is fine?" I said, "Yeah." He said, "Well, most of the copyboys find him very demanding and very tough to work for." I said, "Mr. Walsh, while I was in the Army, I was on General Mark Clark's staff for

The Roosevelt Theatre on State Street, looking north towards Randolph during subway construction in 1941 (courtesy of the Chicago Transit Authority).

nine months. This doesn't bother me at all working for Kup."

I was with Kup for a year and a half at the *Sun-Times*. After I got through in 1958, I opened my own public relations agency at 32 W. Randolph Street. But during those years, I still saw Kup two or three times a week because I was giving him items for his column. We would go out in the evening and make the rounds. It was amazing that of all the people I would meet while I was working, everybody thought that I still worked at the newspaper. I remained close friends with Kup for the rest of his life.

One day, Mr. Balaban called over to the State-Lake Theatre and he wanted to know if I was there and, if so, for me to come upstairs. I walked into his office and met a man named Charlie Levy, the national director of publicity and advertising for Buena Vista, the Walt Disney Company. All of a sudden, Mr. Levy looked at Mr. Balaban, and Mr. Balaban said, "I'd like you to hire Jerry Field!" I had no experience at all doing advertising since I had just graduated from Roosevelt University. Charlie said to me, "Well, the job is for six weeks." I looked at Mr. Balaban, and he winked at me, and I said, "That will be just fine." Mr. Balaban said, "Jerry will have a leave of absence from Balaban and Katz for as long as he works for you." I stayed with Charlie for 2 1/2 years, and my territory was Cleveland, Denver, and as far south as Kansas City. In my first year, I was on the road 48 weeks a year doing promotional work for all the Disney films. As a result, I got ten years of experience in one year of work.

I was negotiating advertising budgets, setting up publicity programs, and doing promotional work.

Television was just starting in 1956, and all of the big movie theatres were still located up and down State Street and around the Loop, including the Chicago Theatre, State-Lake Theatre, Roosevelt Theatre, United Artists Theatre, Woods Theatre, Oriental Theatre, and RKO Palace Theatre. When I finished working for Disney, I wanted to go to work for a newspaper. I couldn't get a job because I didn't have any newspaper experience, except for being a copy boy. I had been freelancing with Al Milton, a publicist who was doing public relations for the Chez Paree, Waikiki Harry's, and four or five other nightclubs. My first publicity client was Frank Harder, the bandleader at the Ivanhoe Restaurant owned by the Jensens. Al had made the original call for me to go over to the Tribune to meet Bill Leonard who was the entertainment editor. He told me to invite him out for dinner, but my response was that I couldn't afford to do that. Al told me to tell the Ivanhoe and they will pick up the tab, but be certain to leave a tip for the waiter. It was probably the best advice I ever received on how to do publicity work, which was to leave good tips for the service people. So, I picked up Bill, had dinner at the Ivanhoe, interviewed Frank Harder, got a picture for Mr. Leonard, and he ran that picture and story. Al said to me, "Did you get paid for it?" I said, "Yes." He said, "Well, now, you are a real press agent, because any idiot can call himself a press agent. The trick is getting paid for it!"

Robert Markovitz

I was born in Chicago at Michael Reese Hospital in 1919.
Our family lived on the West Side of Chicago until I was a year and a
half old, when we migrated to 7500 South on Vincennes Avenue.
I went to Harvard Elementary School, Parker High School, and then
to art school. Going downtown with my parents, we would get
on a streetcar at 75th and Vincennes. We just took the streetcars
all over; we never had a car.

My earliest remembrance of downtown was going to the
Art Institute. I was amazed at the size of the stairways right
and left, and then on up to the top. There was a famous
El Greco painting up there—I didn't know who he was when
I was a kid. I also recall the great stage shows at the Chicago
Theatre. One time, there was an introduction by someone
backstage saying, "And now ladies and gentlemen, here's
Shirley Temple!" And out comes Eddie Cantor, dressed in
drag as Shirley Temple! I think I was disappointed in seeing
not Shirley Temple but Eddie dressed up as a little girl singing
the song. I found the vaudeville section of the movie theatre
really very exciting—seeing the great bands and the great old
acts, and then seeing a wonderful movie.

The first legitimate show that I ever saw was at the
Harris Theatre. I was a high school student, and we all went
down there to actually see a live performance. It was a comedy called *Leaning on Letty*, starring Charlotte Greenwood.
She was a very tall actress who used to kick her legs way up
in the air. I felt so grown up; I'll never forget that.

I was drafted into the army and served in combat in the
70th Division 275th Regiment in Alsace, France. I was married
in 1944 and went overseas a month after my wedding, so
I sorely missed my wife! I spent a year and a half overseas.
After the war was over, I went into show business in a battalion
show and was transferred from the 70th Division to the 3rd
Division, where I continued my show business career as a GI.
In 1946, when I found out I was going to be discharged from
the army, I was surprised but very happy. I took a Liberty Ship
back to New York. Being on the deck and seeing the Statue of
Liberty was a wonderful experience.

When I got out of the army, my first job was working at
Mandel Brothers in the housewares department, and one of
my co-workers was Shelley Berman. We used to have a lot of
fun making jokes, and I was amazed at how when he smiled,
his eyes closed! He was very funny, and that was before he
became successful – he was a student of the stage and we
had a lot of fun making jokes on the floor of Mandel Brothers
while selling pots and pans. On our way up!

Then, I got a job as an apprentice at an art studio doing
paste-ups. In those days, young artists could get jobs that
didn't pay anything, but you could apprentice with artists
who were actually doing commercial artwork. It just so
happened that my first job as an artist was with an old family
friend, whom I admired as a kid because he could draw
wonderful pictures.

After working for the studio on salary, I went freelance,
which meant that you threw yourself at the mercy of the art
market and hoped to get work. And I guess I was fairly
successful because it kept me busy for years. Commercial art
is what I did, enough to send our kids to school and watch
my elder son Mitch go into the railroad business.

Chicago was quite a hub for advertising for a lot of
studios and advertising agencies on Michigan Avenue, Ohio
Street and Grand Avenue, and it was a very busy time. There
were lots of artists and businesses involved with advertising:
Typesetting, photostats...I drew the souvenir map that was
handed out at the Prudential Building observation tower!

I think it's the people that make Chicago's downtown
unique; talk about friendly people! And I'm glad to see a lot
happening with theatre, once again.

The State Street entrance to Mandel Brothers' department store during its 100th Anniversary celebration in 1955 (photographer and publication unknown).

Mandel Brothers' main floor shortly after installation of overhead air conditioning ducts in the late 1940s (courtesy of the Chicago History Museum, ICHi-18962).

Potter Palmer IV

I was born in 1934 and lived in the city until I was 25 years old. I grew up on the Near North Side around Astor and Goethe. My parents and grandparents had their own apartments at 1260 Astor Street and 1301 Astor Street, respectively, across the street from each other which, I think, were built in the early years of the Depression as co-ops. My great grandfather and great grandmother had built a famous mansion in the 1800s on Lake Shore Drive which was sold in the 1930s to a gentleman who later defaulted on the mortgage which my family had given him, so we got the property back.

After WWII, it was sold and residential buildings were constructed on the site. I still love to drive down Astor Street and State Street because it brings back childhood memories.

As for downtown State Street, I don't have many early memories of going there. My grandfather had an office in the old Railway Exchange Building at the corner of Jackson and Michigan Avenue. He would be driven down there in the mornings around 9:30 A.M. or 10 A.M. by a chauffeur. Once in a while, I would run across Astor from 1260 to 1301 and ride down and back with the chauffeur.

I went to the Boys' Latin School when it was originally located on Dearborn. There was also a Girls' Latin School on Scott Street, two blocks west of Lake Shore Drive, where my sister Posy went to school. In fact, the classes for my first two years of dancing school were held at the girls' school. On Saturdays, my friends and I from Latin and Francis Parker School would get lunch at a hamburger place called O'Connell's on the corner of Bellevue and Rush Street where, as one might expect, we would have a hamburger (costing $.39) and a Coke. Then we would all go to the movies at the Esquire Theatre on Oak Street. Very often, we didn't even know what movie was playing. There was usually a newsreel and a cartoon shown along with the movie, and we all used to sit in the same seats each week. Once in a while, we would walk over to the Surf Theatre at Clark and Division to see movies, but, sadly, both the Esquire and the Surf are no longer in business.

The other regular thing we used to do in the mid-1940s was go to Division, east of State, where there was a cigarette shop called Godair's. There, for a dime, one could buy a comic book.

As an early teenager, I didn't go downtown too much. Sometimes, on Sunday afternoons following lunch at grandmother's apartment at 1301 Astor, we would all take a taxi downtown to see a movie. Films were also shown on Sunday afternoons at the Chicago Historical Society at North and Clark, and we would go there once in a while. As I got older, I would also go downtown with my pals by bus to the State-Lake, Chicago, Roosevelt, Oriental, or United Artists Theatres. What I do remember about the Chicago Theatre was that during the summer there was a banner hanging down from the three sides of the marquee that said, in bold letters, "It's Cool Inside." This was before air conditioning was widespread, so it was quite a treat in the summer. There were stage shows interspersed with the movies that were wonderful. Another childhood memory I have was that on the northeast corner of State and Randolph, above the Walgreen's, was a large sign with an advertisement for cigarettes. As part of the picture of a person's face on the sign, there was a circular hole where the mouth was and smoke would come out in the shape of the letter "O" like a smoke ring.

As a kid, we used to go downtown to look at the windows at Marshall Field's during Christmas, an important part of our holiday season. Other times, we would to go to the Palmer House to see the shows at the Empire Room. My grandmother would pile us into her car, and usually we were seated at a table in a very good location. I remember that one time there was a singer named Dorothy Shay, who appeared to be a "sophisticated" country western singer. I had developed a crush on her because she was tall, beautiful, and blond. Somebody snitched on me about my attraction to her, and I remember sitting right on the edge of the dance floor when she came over in the middle of her act and gave me a kiss on my forehead. In response, I turned bright red. I also remember seeing Jimmy Durante and Xavier Cugat there. My family would also go downtown occasionally in the evening to the theatre.

top
Looking west on Madison from atop The Boston Store
in 1936. The Morrison Hotel is visible at left
(courtesy of the Chicago Transit Authority).

bottom
Madison Street looking west from Clark in 1935
(courtesy of the Chicago Transit Authority).

following page
State Street looking north from Van Buren c. 1936.
Photographer and publication unknown (Copyright by
Chicago Sun-Times, Inc. Reprinted with permission).

The Downtown That Time Forgot

Picture postcards and tourist brochures of the 1930s and 1940s invariably promoted the finest sights and institutions that downtown Chicago had to offer. But, not surprisingly, the less compelling fringe neighborhood surrounding downtown's main shopping, entertainment, and financial core was ignored. These blocks contained mostly factories and warehouses, together with modest storefront businesses that served factory workers and the flow of pedestrian traffic between the Loop and railroad stations.

Of particular note is the locale immediately south of the Van Buren Street leg of the Loop "L," best known for a stretch of long, narrow blocks on either side of Dearborn Street where printing and publishing firms constructed factory buildings in the late 19th and early 20th centuries. Today, of course, this area is known as Printer's Row. But surrounding this district was a sea of parking lots, undistinguished buildings, and struggling small businesses.

This area, together with the rest of downtown, was rebuilt shortly after the Great Fire. It initially prospered due to its closeness to several railroad terminals and their booming passenger and freight traffic. Hotels and eateries were built to accommodate passengers and crews in transit. Companies needing close proximity to rail corridors found ample quarters in nearby loft buildings.

But, just to the north, skyscraper construction and the allure of a more prestigious address drew larger and more prosperous retail and commercial businesses into the burgeoning Loop district. Despite lower rents in the fringe areas, a rundown and seedy atmosphere hinting at an earlier era of crooked politics and organized crime repelled all but the most hardscrabble entrepreneurs. In the 1950s, construction of the Congress Expressway eliminated some of the blight by cutting a wide swath through this area, but otherwise redevelopment did not arrive at Printer's Row until the late 1970s. Not until the 1990s did renewal finally begin to extend to the surrounding area, bridging the gap between downtown and the up-and-coming South Loop neighborhood.

It would be inappropriate to dismiss this obscure and neglected district, which remained stagnant for over half a century, as a slum or skid row. The offices and factories were a respectable and important adjunct to Chicago's commerce, and the men who resided in the squalid hotels surely helped to sustain the marginal storefront businesses. The streets and buildings may have appeared less than inviting; nonetheless, this neighborhood served as a gateway and was thus an integral part of downtown Chicago.

The images shown on these pages were stored for decades in dusty binders labeled "West Route Superhighway." Originally proposed by Daniel Burnham in his 1909 Plan and built as the Congress Expressway, this road is known today as Interstate 290 or the Eisenhower Expressway. When project planning began in the late 1930s (the actual start of construction was delayed until after World War II), Congress Street was not a through street. To permit extending and widening Congress between Michigan Avenue and Franklin Street, the city had to acquire and condemn several buildings. In the earliest stages of planning, they hired professional photographers to document existing property parcels along the route for valuation purposes.

Surely the photographers and engineers who unwittingly assembled these photos had no idea of their eventual historic value. But these candid and unpretentious images, long forgotten and literally fished out of a Dumpster, capture a moment in time. In stark contrast to the much more upscale central core of downtown, they portray the gritty essence of everyday life in "the downtown that time forgot."

The Hotel Northern Pacific at 442 South Sherman Street, photographed in 1939, was dwarfed by the Insurance Exchange Building in the background. This railroad hotel, built in the exotic Moorish style in 1888, was demolished in 1948 to clear a path for construction of the Congress Expressway (Copelin photo, Eric Bronsky Collection).

Congress Street, looking east towards the Congress & Wabash "L" station (since removed) and the Auditorium Building in 1948. Originally a narrow and rather sleepy side street between Michigan and State, Congress would soon be widened and extended west to feed into the Congress expressway (Eric Bronsky Collection).

Pedestrians walk past Sears' display windows on State Street. The State & Van Buren Loop "L" station in the background was demolished in the 1970s (Eric Bronsky Collection).

next page
A family strolls west on Congress at Wabash. Anne's was a familiar chain of Loop steak restaurants and lounges in the 1940s (Eric Bronsky Collection).

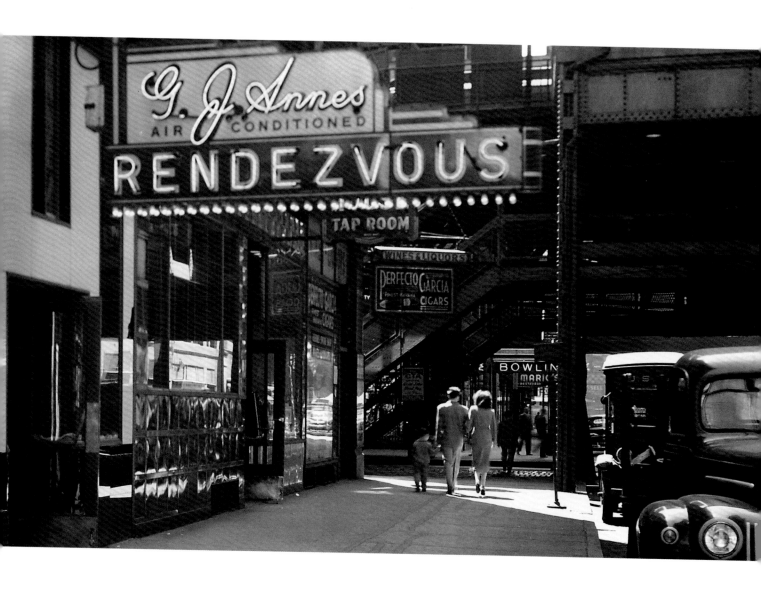

left page, top left
South and west of the Sears block, the character of the surrounding area changed abruptly. A seedy collection of shops including taverns, liquor and tobacco stores, pawnshops, and the Loop Gospel Mission at 17-19 E. Congress were clustered around the intersection of State and Congress (Eric Bronsky Collection).

left page, top right
Interior of the Congress Cigar & Liquor Store at 23-39 E. Congress (Eric Bronsky Collection).

left page, bottom
Around the corner on State was a men's clothing store where Arrow shirts cost $1.29 and 5 pairs of socks could be had for a dollar (Eric Bronsky Collection).

Burlesque houses still existed in the South Loop in 1941. The art deco Gem Theatre at 450 S. State and the streamlined Babbette's Lounge next door reflected design trends stemming from the Century of Progress Exposition (Eric Bronsky Collection).

The dressing room on the second floor of the Gem Theatre. This business' high standards were exemplified by a sign reading, "All girls will please use DEODORANT before going on duty" (Eric Bronsky Collection).

top left
The building at 500-510 S. State housed a variety of small storefront businesses, and upstairs was the Regal Hotel for Men. According to signs, rooms that were "newly decorated, comfortably furnished and clean" could be rented for 30¢ a night (Eric Bronsky Collection).

top right
The "Yes Yes Club" at 452-54 S. State had a drop ceiling and concealed ventilation ductwork, a rarity in 1941. Its stylish interior was strikingly modern even by today's standards (Eric Bronsky Collection).

bottom
The Pennyland Arcade enticed conventioneers and servicemen with a variety of amusements that included a shooting gallery, photo booths and the Vibro-Pep machine, which "stimulates circulation and relieves foot fatigue" (Eric Bronsky Collection).

top

The pawnshop at 456 S. State featured jewelry and musical instruments; the luggage and fur departments were located on the balcony in the back of the store (Eric Bronsky Collection).

center

Conveniently located next to the hotel entrance, the Pink Poodle attracted conventioneers attending events at the nearby Coliseum with their "All Girl Revue" (Eric Bronsky Collection).

bottom

The anchor store in this building was Radio Doctors Inc., which sold and serviced radios. An extensive array of vacuum tubes and parts is visible behind the counter at right. Private booths where customers could listen to radios and recordings lined the wall at left (Eric Bronsky Collection).

left page, above left
West of Dearborn Street, buildings and businesses such as this walkup at
504-12 S. Clark appeared even more derelict and woebegone than those on
South State Street (Eric Bronsky Collection).

left page, above right
The stove-heated interior of the Shanghai Restaurant was bereft of décor
between the stamped tin ceiling and peeling linoleum (Eric Bronsky Collection).

left page, center left
Above the restaurant were apartments. This bedroom was typical for a
family that was struggling to make ends meet in the later years of the
Depression (Eric Bronsky Collection).

left page, center right
The lobby of this SRO (single room occupancy) men's hotel at
440-44 S. Clark was photographed in 1940, but this scene is archetypical of
the Depression era (Eric Bronsky Collection).

left page, bottom
SRO accommodations were very basic cubicles with chicken wire ceilings.
Barely large enough to fit a cot, the only amenity was a bare light bulb
dangling from a wire (Eric Bronsky Collection).

above
A warehouse and manufacturing district dominated the west and southwest
fringes of the Loop. This 1949 view looks northeast from the South Branch
of the Chicago River at Van Buren Street. The Dearborn Street Subway
had not yet been completed and the old Logan Square, Garfield and Douglas
rapid transit routes still entered the Loop "L" through a junction at Van Buren
and Wells (Eric Bronsky Collection).

Ann Roth

When I first came to Northwestern University back in the early '40s, the Loop was really a viable, exciting place to visit. Wabash Avenue was particularly an inviting spot, with such stores as Marshall Field's, Carson's, the Fair, Colby's Furniture Store, and Joseph's Shoe Store. Across downtown, there were numerous places to eat like Stouffer's, Henrici's, the Walnut Room at Field's, Fritzel's, Shangri-La, the Italian Village, Berghoff's, and of course, my husband Don's Blackhawk Restaurant. The movie theatres and legitimate theatres were only a short walk from many of these restaurants.

Coming to town on the comfortable North Shore Line from Evanston in those days, for me, was a real adventure. It was so much easier than taking the "L" (the North Shore Line was much more comfortable) or even driving downtown since the Edens Highway hadn't been built. The evenings offered tremendous entertainment too, because most of the major hotels and big restaurants had live orchestras and dancing.

The Blackhawk Restaurant was opened in 1920 by Don's father, Otto Roth. We are uncertain why he chose that location on Wabash for the restaurant, but it may have been because that particular real estate was available. The restaurant business was a risky proposition in the 1920s and got even riskier by the 1930s and the Great Depression. The location of Marshall Field's just west of the restaurant may have been a factor in the selection of the site. It was just a hotbed and very busy commercial area, and Wabash and Randolph was just a block from the Chicago Theatre. There was string orchestra music played upstairs at the Blackhawk before Don's father had jazz orchestras that did national radio broadcasts. The Blackhawk was also well known for the many famous big bands that performed there.

In fact, there was music played for the first New Year's Eve celebration they had at the restaurant. It included a cover charge, dinner, and dancing until 2 A.M. for just $1.50 per person. Musical groups were traveling the country in the 1920s, and the Blackhawk was one of the locales where the groups performed; it was one of the earliest restaurants to combine food with broadcast music. At that time, Chicago also had the Trianon and Aragon Ballrooms where people could go to hear music and dance. In addition, the Sherman House, the Chez Paree, and even some of the movie houses had live entertainment. The Loop was booming with activity.

Don was continually creating new ideas to keep people coming to the Loop. He had buses that took restaurant patrons to the legitimate theatres and the Lyric Opera. He also exhibited beautiful art in the restaurant with the collections furnished by local galleries. After Don no longer had orchestras, there were many, many small musicals at the restaurant which he produced with professionals from Broadway.

In the '50s, '60s, and '70s, Chicago was the kingpin for tourism. Most of the large conventions were held here because we were the railroad hub of the country, and the Loop literally thrived on this. Slowly, though, the scene began to change because North Michigan Avenue, across the bridge over the Chicago River, started to take hold and some of the better stores began to move northward. The stores along Wabash Avenue and State Street felt the pinch and began to close. These included the Fair, Colby's, and Rothschild's, and even the venerable old Marshall Field's seemed to have changed, and, with it, the store's clientele. As air travel grew and expanded across the country, other cities started to take away some of Chicago's convention business. This was a real blow to business in the Loop.

BLACKHAWK
ESTAURANT
"LAUGH IT OFF"
W YORK MUSICAL COMEDY
BRANDON & ORCHESTRA
LUNCHEON SERVED DAILY
INJUNBAR
INDIAN ROOM
EASTMAN Kodak STORES Co.
Kodaks

Don sensed all of these changes and felt that it was time
to make some decisions about the Blackhawk. We owned the
building in which the Blackhawk Restaurant resided. In fact,
on many occasions, Don tried to buy the property that was
connected northward to the corner, thinking that perhaps we
might develop the project commercially. Unfortunately, he
wasn't able to make that purchase. However, an offer came
along to purchase our property which Don just couldn't resist
and he decided to sell. The Blackhawk building needed major
repairs at that time and operating a 500-600 seat restaurant
in the Loop was becoming risky business, all of which added
to Don's decision to sell.

I often heard Don say that if there were any one thing
that contributed to the demise of the Loop, it would probably
be the assassination of Dr. Martin Luther King in April 1968
and the burning of the area west of the Loop. It was truly
a horrifying experience for Chicago. Don felt that the event
terrorized the Loop for many years afterward.

Many different groups have tried to put the pieces
together again downtown, like the State Street Mall, Block 37,
and other things like that, but it just didn't happen. However,
there seems to be "a light at the end of the tunnel" with the
building of the beautiful Millennium Park and the influx of
tourists to see it. Things are looking up, but I think that what
is really great is the building of the large number of condominiums and apartment buildings in and around the downtown
area which certainly seems to be bringing the people back.
Who knows...maybe "the phoenix will rise again!"

top right
Eddie Hubbard, c. 1940 (courtesy, Don Roth's Blackhawk Restaurant)

center left
The Blackhawk was periodically remodeled and always looked fresh and up to date, even in its final days. As published in the *Chicago Sun-Times*. Photographed by Al Seib (Copyright 1984 by Chicago Sun-Times, Inc. Reprinted with permission).

center right
Les Brown and his Band of Renown, c. 1948 (courtesy, Don Roth's Blackhawk Restaurant).

bottom right
Kay Kyser and Kyser's College of Musical Knowledge performing at the Blackhawk c. 1937 (photo courtesy of Harry Thomas, courtesy Don Roth's Blackhawk Restaurant).

next page
One of Don Roth's many creative innovations was the Spinning Salad Bowl, shown here being prepared tableside by Siraj. As published in the *Chicago Sun-Times*. Photographed by Ray Burley (Copyright 1977 by Chicago Sun-Times, Inc. Reprinted with permission).

A family dining at the Walnut Room in 1947 (M.J. Schmidt photo, courtesy of the Chicago History Museum, ICHi-38786).

The main floor of Marshall Field's was bustling with holiday shoppers in December, 1968 (Gustav D. Frank photo, courtesy of the Chicago History Museum, ICHi-51199).

Holiday decorations adorning Field's main floor and atrium in December, 1968 (Gustav D. Frank photo, courtesy of the Chicago History Museum, ICHi-51200).

Christmas at Marshall Field's

To several generations of Chicago children, few holiday traditions surpassed the ritual visit to Marshall Field's to see Santa in person, dine under the tree in the festive Walnut Room, explore the legendary toy department on the fourth floor, and marvel at the elaborate decorations inside the store as well as the window scenes on State Street. Lucile Ward Robinson, a WPA muralist and artist who worked for Marshall Field's in the early 1950s, was responsible for designing and decorating many of those very special displays. The story of her creativity and her family's involvement in the store's ever-changing seasonal displays is told by her daughter, Mary Robinson Kalista.

Mary Robinson Kalista

Marshall Field's had two separate departments: Interior Display and Window Display. Both departments did similar things and were comprised of artists and assistants. One department took care of the artwork within the store, and the other did the windows. My mother was originally hired to make ornaments for the main Christmas tree in the Walnut Room, and then she also helped with the decorations for the State Street Christmas windows.

After that, she worked in the window display department and was permanently assigned to do the 28 Shop windows on the Washington Street side of the store. Eventually, she moved to the interior display department where she did the fourth floor escalator cases, Cozy Cloud Cottage, Candy Cane Lane, and the Christmas Narcissus Room Fountain.

My mother was the designer; she was the one who would come up with all the ideas and she would make complete scale drawings of everything. Sometimes she would get ideas from my father, who was a builder, architect, and general Renaissance man. And sometimes my brother and I would be in on it, too, giving her our ideas. The store had a whole crew of painters and carpenters, many of whom had come from Germany where they had apprenticed in carpentry, painting, draping, and upholstery. They would cut things out and build and assemble the displays according to her instructions. Then, they or my mother would paint everything and she would add the finishing touches, special murals, pasted decorations, trim, etc. What couldn't be made in-house was sent out to display houses such as Silvestri, Stengaard, and others.

The workshop was well equipped with every imaginable art supply. Some items were created new while others were reused from old displays. For example, wooden elf figures hand carved by Karl Halshammer, a German wood carver who worked for Stengaard and was fairly well known in Chicago, could turn up in a lot of different displays as either elves or angels, depending on how they were dressed and decorated.

Animated figures have always fascinated children. Field's did use a fair amount of mechanical animation back in those days, and anything that had to be mechanized was made by companies like Silvestri. Although some pre-made displays were available, my mother would design her own and the display houses would build them from her exact scale drawings. Of course, now in Macy's windows, everything is just designed and produced by outside display companies.

And the deadlines were hideous! For example, when my mother did Cozy Cloud Cottage, she started it in the summer, but the night before it had to be finished, she worked with the wallpaper hangers until 2 in the morning, took a taxi home to Hyde Park, slept for a couple of hours, got up, showered, re-dressed, and came back downtown for the opening. We were very little, but during those times, she used to work late every night, getting home at 8 or 9.

Since a considerable amount of time and money were spent to produce these elaborate displays, my mother felt that it was important to preserve them in some way. So, she hired people to take photographs of her work for her personal files. These images provide a historical record of all of the displays that my mother designed during her time at Marshall Field's.

Marshall Field's holiday decorations at State and Washington in December, 2005. (Eric Bronsky photo).

The year is 1955, and we're standing in the main aisle of Candy Cane Lane on the fourth floor. This entire floor was the children's department—clothing, shoes, and toys. Naturally, they called this Candy Cane Lane because every year at Christmastime they decorated the pillar areas above the cases where the toys were with large candy canes. The theme here was the festival of lights—on each column there was an angel lighting Christmas lights in some fashion, and as you looked down the aisle, the decorative lighting made it appear all very magical. Below, you can see all the cases of toys, dolls, and trains. This was paradise for a child. We spent untold hours in this area.

Here's a closer look at the marvelous detail work on one of the columns in Candy Cane Lane. There was a different scene on each column. Workers normally installed seasonal displays while the store was open for business, but with Christmas displays, I think they generally tried to work at night and also keep things fairly hidden, maybe covered in drapes, until everything was finished. The displays would probably be unveiled on the same day Cozy Cloud Cottage opened, which I seem to recall was the Saturday after Thanksgiving. Santa arrived in the Thanksgiving Day parade and then took up residence at Cozy Cloud Cottage—at least that's what we all believed!

bottom left

The 1954 theme for Candy Cane Lane featured Santa preparing to take off on his Christmas Eve journey, so this column shows the elves loading the sleigh with gifts.
To the right, you have Aunt Holly who, together with Uncle Mistletoe, were Marshall Field's own Christmas characters created in 1946 by Johanna Osborne, head of the Window Display Department.

top right

On the fourth floor, there were three escalator display cases. They were somewhat similar to the store windows but without glass, and they were the first things you would see as you stepped off the escalator. This is a Christmas display from 1954. The little girls hear a noise, wake up and turn on the light, and Santa hides because he doesn't want to be seen!

Since the escalator cases were rather shallow, the bed had to be foreshortened and Santa had to be made relatively flat, creating the illusion of perspective when viewed from the front.

bottom right

Here's another escalator case where depth is an illusion. This scene is a Christmas banquet. Santa's elves are bringing the food in on trays, and Santa himself is carving the turkey. If you look closely at the chair backs, you can see that they resemble angel wings. Again, because the display area is so shallow, the elements in the foreground are three-dimensional but the scene is carried further back with the table, its settings, and many more figures in the form of cutouts on the back wall. We still have the wheel light fixture with little angels holding candles at our house!

Besides hiring photographers to capture her elaborate displays for posterity, my mother also wrote detailed notes about the displays in diary fashion. I'll let her describe the creation of Cozy Cloud Cottage in her own words:

"In 1953, I was given this thrilling assignment: I was simply given a floor plan of the house and large area out in front. I presented my overall design to Mr. John Moss [executive in charge of all displays] for approval in June. Then, with a budget of about $15,000, I started work on producing it.

"I worked on getting things built and made during July, August, and September. The Trend House was then closed to the public, and work began there building, painting, and installing everything. The sky was almost the limit as to what I could do. I had the finest of carpenters, painters, and electricians at my disposal, but of course, I had to give them very careful working drawings in scale for every detail.

"For that year's version, I decided to locate Santa Claus's house at the North Pole, surrounded by the beautiful lights of the Aurora Borealis. Then, I keyed my color scheme to these pastel colors. Over the entire top of the house in the distance, I had panels painted in rays of pastel colors, covered them with glitter, and had lights gradually going on and off over them.

"I wanted to use carrier pigeons to carry airmail letters to Santa from children all over the world. So, flying over the maze [the area in front of the house where people waited] were 24 large white doves all carrying letters in their bills. In the garden in front of the cottage was a large four-strip landing field (surrounded by snow), but the strips themselves were laid out in four pastel colored sands. The white doves also had reflections of these colors on their feathers, and each dove presumably landed on the strip that matched its own color. Nearby was the control tower from which an elf directed them to land. Santa's red stocking cap (with white fur) provided the windsock to show the direction of the wind."

next page
Here is the interior of Cozy Cloud Cottage in 1953. Of course, Santa sat in the red chair, his telescope within easy reach. Behind his chair was a window with a view of the Aurora Borealis, and next to the chair was his book of good girls and boys. We especially loved that because our names and those of some of our friends appeared prominently. Above the hearth was the legend, "Be good, and you'll be happy." The portraits of Santa's reindeer, each done in velvet with names in gold letters, appear on the walls. Every piece, large and small, was drawn to scale and made individually; there are so many details!

During the rest of the year, Cozy Cloud Cottage was actually the Trend House, which displayed modern furniture in a home-like setting. In later years, it was reduced to just one room. But this was the original Trend House, and you had to go through two or three rooms before you got to Santa. For kids, a visit to Field's Santa was one of the prime memories; it was almost bigger than lunch at the Walnut Room under the big tree. We waited in huge, long maze lines outside of this cottage—with thousands going through it every day; you might easily wait an hour to see Santa. But there were lots of fun things going on. There was a snow-covered garden with reindeer. My mother designed male and female birds that were made by a display company; out on the corner of the porch of the house was perched a magnificent, imaginary, large, fantastic bird, which my mother called a "Polar Bird of Paradise." Hidden down in the roof was a tape recording of a bird song. This song was repeated at intervals to make it sound like the bird was singing to its mate on the nest in the adjoining tree.

The tree was really a large permanent column disguised as a gigantic tree. The trunk was covered with crinkled silver foil painted white to appear like bark. At the top, my mother had ordered 20-foot tree limbs, which were attached near the top of the trunk and to the ceiling, spreading in all directions. These were spray painted white with pastel tones of lavender, green, pink, and yellow here and there. The entire tree was covered with fruit—large round Christmas ornaments sprayed in these same colors, and she called those "Aurora Apples."

There was also a large igloo, which was cut in half so that you could see what was going on inside. On the right side, little angels were preparing cookies, making and dressing dolls, and wrapping presents for all the good little girls. And on the left side, little elves were making trains and other toys for the good little boys. At the bottom center you had two elves who were turning a little winch that would make Santa rise up out of a pole (the North Pole) in the center of the igloo, take his telescope in hand, turn and look for the good boys and girls, and then come back down.

This scene, also located in the waiting area just outside the cottage, featured an angel choir.

When you exited the Cottage, there was the "Penguin Drive-in & Snack Bar." Here, penguins were sitting on stools along a bar being serving by jolly elf figures. On the bar were clever signs like "Formal attire required," "Please don't honk for service," and "One honk and you're out." There was also a very clever menu which had items like "Polar Pola," "Eskimo Pie," "Frosted Bear Claws," "Iced Icicles," and many more.

This classical marble fountain was the centerpiece of the Narcissus Room, one of the tea rooms on the seventh floor. Not everyone is aware that all of the dining rooms in Field's had fancy Christmas decorations.

The fountain had an upper basin supported by six caryatids standing in a large lower basin. During the year, water flowed from the upper to the lower basin. But during the holidays, strings of white lights formed a Christmas tree reaching toward the sky and lighting a nativity scene crèche just below. The caryatids, dressed like angels, support this tree and crèche. The base of the fountain form a skating pond where little angels are ice skating, sledding, and delivering presents—some are portrayed with crooks and little wooly sheep like those often seen in German Christmas villages. This fountain, elegantly sophisticated when viewed from afar, actually is a combination of many happy aspects of Christmas for children and adults alike.

left
The Narcissus fountain in December, 2005 (Eric Bronsky photo).

Dining under the Christmas tree at the Walnut Room in December 2005
(Eric Bronsky photo).

A "green hornet" streetcar heads south on State Street past Marshall Field's in the fifties (William C. Hoffman photo, Wien-Criss Archive).

View south from the observation deck of the Prudential Building.
showing the Illinois Central Railroad tracks, Grant Park,
Art Institute and Michigan Avenue in 1963 (Charles Cushman
Collection, Indiana University Archives P12889).

below
Looking north towards the Loop "L" junction at Wabash and Van Buren. North Shore Line's Electroliners were surely the most unique trains to ever operate on the Loop "L." These fast and comfortable streamliners made five round trips per day between Chicago and Milwaukee, and had a lounge car that served beverages and light meals (Pete Busack photo, Ed Halstead Collection).

next page, top left
Clark Street looking north towards the Loop "L" at Van Buren on a very smoggy morning in the fifties. (William C. Hoffman photo, Wien-Criss Archive).

next page, center left
A "green hornet" streetcar southbound on Clark Street at Madison in the fifties. Wimpy's, the Clark Theatre and the Hotel Planters were replaced by Three First National Plaza in 1981 (William C. Hoffman photo, Wien-Criss Archive).

next page, bottom
Looking northeast from the main Post Office at Van Buren and the South Branch of the Chicago River, a Chicago Aurora & Elgin interurban train heads east on the old West Side elevated route in the early fifties. This route was later replaced by a rapid transit line in the median of the Congress Expressway. The CA&E RR linked Chicago with communities along the Fox River and intermediate suburbs from 1902 until 1957 (courtesy Electric Railway Historical Society Collection).

next page, top right
Wabash Avenue looking north at Harrison in 1951. A northbound North Shore Line train is on the "L." The Chicago North Shore & Milwaukee Railroad shared rapid transit routes and facilities into downtown Chicago from 1919 until 1963 (William E. Robertson photo, Eric Bronsky Collection).

next page, center right
A northbound Electroliner glides past a cluster of music stores on its approach to the Adams & Wabash station in the early sixties (Joseph M. Canfield photo, Eric Bronsky Collection).

following page
A train of preserved 1922-vintage rapid transit cars heads west on Van Buren at State, past the former Goldblatt's department store building (Eric Bronsky photo).

"Our downtown is unique from other cities because of the idea that someone has drawn a circle called the Loop."
Gary Johnson

"A lot of people felt that the Loop "L" structure was a city landmark. It so identified Chicago that if you removed it we would have lost a major element of what made Chicago different from any other major city."
Jim O'Connor

PART III
THE CONSTRUCTION
BOOM
1950s-1970s

The Construction Boom

The migration of families to Chicago from other parts of the country, which began during the Depression, accelerated throughout the postwar boom years. As the local economy perked up, job opportunities continued to expand. African-Americans seeking better prospects for employment, and perceiving less racial discrimination than in the southern states, were arriving in record numbers. By the early 1950s, it became apparent that Chicago's population growth would soon exceed the supply of available housing.

Since there was no appreciable amount of vacant land in Chicago and redevelopment of blighted neighborhoods during that era was synonymous with subsidized public housing projects for the poor, construction of new housing for the middle class pushed out beyond the city limits into adjoining semirural areas. Developments closest to existing or proposed transportation corridors linking the suburbs to downtown were clearly the most sought after.

Most buyers of new suburban properties were not new arrivals to the area, but rather inner-city residents who felt compelled to move due to changing needs and neighborhood demographics. The evolving inner-city neighborhoods and the explosive growth of the suburbs and their automobile culture initiated a chain of events that would ultimately have a profound impact on downtown.

Meanwhile, construction of new buildings downtown had gradually resumed. The clean lines and absence of ornamentation espoused in the designs of modernist architects like Mies van der Rohe were now the rage, and earlier architectural styles quickly fell out of favor. The rise of the starkly modern Prudential Building in a highly visible location heralded the replacement of many antiquated buildings with the more lucrative skyscrapers.

Newly prosperous Chicagoans seemed overly anxious to shed anything that even vaguely recalled the gloom and doom of the Depression and war years. This purge extended beyond prewar architecture to material things like antique furniture and lifestyle considerations, including dependency upon public transportation. Combined with the

zeal of investors and developers intent on making their fortunes through demolishing obsolete downtown properties and building anew, the face of downtown began to change dramatically.

By the mid-sixties, construction cranes dotted the Loop. Single structures were taken down at first, but piecemeal demolition gradually expanded into redeveloping entire city blocks. Downtown buildings that would have been considered historical landmarks by present-day standards fell to the wrecking ball and were replaced with steel, concrete, and glass boxes. By the time the historic preservation movement finally picked up momentum in the seventies, many irreplaceable treasures were sadly lost.

It should be noted that nearly all of the redeveloped blocks had previously hosted diverse tenants and usages—manufacturing, office, retail, hotel, and entertainment. The older buildings were pedestrian-friendly in that they housed an assortment of family-owned retail stores and restaurants with direct sidewalk access. But the new office towers were basically single-use. They had austere glassed-in street-level lobbies with little or no frontage set aside for stores or restaurants. Any shops and dining venues were there primarily for the convenience of tenants; these were usually located deep inside the buildings, invisible to passersby. As rebuilding progressed, Loop streets that were once lively in the evening fell silent after office workers departed for the day.

Planners and architects gradually realized the importance of retaining some open space in the form of street-level plazas. At first, these were intended primarily for esthetic considerations—to break up the solid concentration of blocky buildings and provide more light and space. The advent of amenities to convert these barren plazas into inviting public spaces did not occur until years later. Traffic congestion remained a thorny issue. During the fifties, several Loop streets were converted to one-way streets, traffic lanes were distinctly marked, and street lighting and signals were vastly improved. Ongoing improvements to Lake Shore Drive enhanced vehicular access from the North and South Sides, and the opening of the first segment of the Congress Expressway in 1956 provided a more expedient route from the city's West Side and western suburbs. Such improved access encouraged more people to eschew public transportation and drive downtown for both business and pleasure. The express highway system originally proposed in the 1909 *Plan of Chicago* and designed prior to World War II was ultimately completed by 1964.

The Dearborn Subway, delayed by the war and finally completed in 1951, added further capacity to the transit system. However, the electric streetcars that had ably transported generations of Chicagoans to school, work, shopping, and leisure activities tragically succumbed to what city legislators believed was progress. Although modernization had begun under a CTA predecessor, much of the fleet along with the track and overhead wire needed extensive renewal or replacement. Wooed by the notions that buses were cheaper to implement and more flexible than fixed rail routes, and urged by those who viewed traditional streetcars as a hindrance to vehicular traffic flow, the CTA converted the streetcar lines to bus one by one. The last streetcar to operate in Chicago rolled into the carbarn on June 22, 1958.

As suburbs continued to develop, the convenience of brand new regional shopping centers whose department stores were basically full-service branches of their State Street counterparts lured shoppers away from downtown. Moreover, North Michigan Avenue just across the river was becoming a more fashionable shopping destination and a growing number of high-end stores chose to locate there rather than in the Loop. So, it was no surprise when retail business on State Street began to erode. The Boston Store succumbed to competition in 1948, and two more once-fashionable department stores that had been downtown Chicago fixtures since the mid-1800s were sold to less upscale successors: Mandel Brothers became Wieboldt's in 1960, and The Fair Store was extensively remodeled and reopened as Montgomery Ward in 1964.

Due in large part to the advent of commercial jet aircraft in the early sixties, air travel became more popular than long-distance rail travel and the importance of the railroad passenger terminals downtown declined precipitously. Hotel and convention facilities built near O'Hare Airport siphoned off much of the business that had been the lifeblood of the downtown hotels. Badly in need of refurbishment, the towering Morrison Hotel at the southwest corner of Madison and Dearborn was one of the first casualties, and the LaSalle Hotel and Sherman House were among other well-known hotels to close within the next decade.

Even though both of these photos were taken from the same general vantage point—on Randolph, looking east towards Michigan—the images are separated by over thirty years. The old wood and steel truss bridge over the IC tracks was replaced by a wider and much sturdier viaduct in the thirties, but more obvious in the 1954 view is the steel framework for the Prudential building. The main Chicago Public Library is at right, across the street from Pixley & Ehlers' Restaurant (both photos, courtesy of the Chicago Transit Authority).

left

With more people commuting downtown by auto, finding a place to park became more of a challenge. This 1953 view of Michigan Boulevard looking north from Adams shows the Grant Park Underground Garage under construction (courtesy of the Chicago Transit Authority).

The garage opened for business long before the Prudential Building (background) was completed, helping to alleviate the parking shortage. In 1954 it cost $2.35 to park here for 24 hours (courtesy of the Chicago History Museum, ICHi-25813).

South Michigan Boulevard remained relatively unchanged in appearance. Though stately and elegant, it never attracted the high-end retail businesses that preferred the thoroughfare north of the Chicago River. As published in the *Chicago Sun-Times*. Photographer: Dave Mann (Copyright 1953 by Chicago Sun-Times, Inc. Reprinted with permission).

Apart from roadway improvements, it was several years before the skyscraper boom would expand to the outer fringes of the Loop and beyond. Several surface parking lots and late 19th century buildings remained standing along this stretch of Wacker Drive between Franklin and Lake into the 1980s. The Civic Opera House was the tallest building in this 1962 scene (courtesy of the Chicago Transit Authority).

By 1956, the Wacker Drive extension and the Congress Expressway's twin bascule bridges were nearing completion. Entire blocks of old South Loop buildings were razed to make room for a cloverleaf interchange connecting the two roadways. The main Post Office building is at bottom left (Eric Bronsky Collection).

This stretch of Clark Street looking north from Van Buren changed relatively little between 1936 (far left) and 1955 (center). (Both photos, courtesy of the Chicago Transit Authority.)

But, here is the exact same location in 2007. Except for the Edison Building in the distance, virtually nothing else is recognizable (Eric Bronsky photo).

Entire blocks of prime Loop real estate were redeveloped. This view shows the southeast corner of Randolph and Dearborn in 1961. Henrici's and other restaurants continued to thrive because they were close to the movie theatres. However, their buildings were becoming decrepit and this block was eyed by Cook County as a suitable site for a new government office building. As published in the *Chicago Sun-Times*. Photographer: Bob Rubel (Copyright 1961 by Chicago Sun-Times, Inc. Reprinted with permission).

In 1965 the Civic Center (renamed Richard J. Daley Center in 1976) was completed on that site. The open space in the form of a pedestrian plaza was a new concept for that time, as was the huge Picasso sculpture unveiled in 1967 (courtesy of the Chicago Transit Authority).

Gary T. Johnson

I was born in 1950, and at that time, my parents were living in Forest Park. But within a few months, we moved to Park Ridge and that was where I grew up. We lived in a couple of different places, one north and one south of Uptown Park Ridge, where the Pickwick Theatre still is. (For us, downtown meant Chicago, and uptown was the central shopping district in Park Ridge.). I think that the trip I remember to downtown Chicago was when my grandmother took my sister and me to Marshall Field's at Christmas.

I still remember what she said to us. "Now, you're going to see a lot of people dressed as Santa Claus, but the only real one is at Marshall Field's." Of course, it was such an amazing experience. I remember that the line was long and that there was a little house where Santa sat, and I remember how the tree soared in the central space at Field's. In fact, I remember that much better than the decorated windows, even though the windows are still iconic for a lot of people. But for me, it was business first, and the business was to go see Santa and make my feelings about Christmas presents known to him.

Another wonderful memory I have was when I was old enough to come downtown by myself. I was doing a report in 1962 when I was in seventh grade. The topic was John Marshall, Chief Justice of the U.S. Supreme Court. So I went to the Main Library and remember finding books that I never dreamed even existed and discovering the concept of being in a palace of learning. I remember leaning back in my chair and trying to read the words that were written in the mosaic tiles on the wall. While sitting in the reading room, I noticed there was a gentleman who sat down next to me who I swore was Buffalo Bill Cody because he had long grey hair and a beard. This was an era of crew cuts, and I thought that I was in the presence of greatness. From then on, I found every reason I could to return to that library whenever I had any kind of theme paper to write. The trip downtown meant that I could

take a Chicago and Northwestern train from Park Ridge and get off at the Northwestern Station on Canal. I had a great uncle who ran the information booth at that station, and people would come from all directions to ask him questions.

Then, there was the time I went to the Michael Todd Cinestage on Dearborn to see *Around The World in Eighty Days* in Todd AO. I was just shocked with the idea that there was such a thing as buying advanced tickets to see a movie. But this wasn't just seeing a movie…it was a whole experience. We had the Pickwick in Park Ridge, so it was rare that we would come downtown to see movies. One of the business accounts that my grandfather, the banker, had was Balaban and Katz Theatres. So, there were lots of pictures in my family of my grandfather being photographed with Barney Balaban, and that made Tom Johnson a celebrity. I always had this image of what downtown was like because my grandfather would dress up in his business suit and a hat each workday. My grandmother would drive him to the train in Park Ridge, and he would join all these other people going downtown. By the time I was born in 1950, my grandfather was reaching the end of his career, but I remember hearing the stories about how he would often sleep through his railroad stop in Park Ridge on his way home from work. As a result, my grandmother would have to drive like crazy to Des Plaines, and, occasionally, to Mount Prospect to get him

following page
Celebrants assembled at State and Wacker to dedicate the new
Bataan-Corregidor Memorial Bridge, better known as State Street Bridge, on
May 28, 1949. Two venerable Loop restaurants, Fritzel's and Shangri-La,
are in the background (Eric Bronsky Collection).

off the train. So, he was part of this group of men who all dressed with similar hats and suits.

As for downtown restaurants, the Blackhawk Restaurant was a favorite eating establishment for one of my great aunts. For a real treat, she would take my sister and me to the Blackhawk and we felt like "kings of the hill." I didn't like salads, so the spinning salad had no particular meaning to me, but I liked the hot roast beef sandwich. I also remember Henrici's very well. Then, there were what appeared to us to be exotic restaurants that my parents would go to with their friends, including Don the Beachcomber and Trader Vic's. The only way we could drink if we joined them there was out of one of the coconuts they bought at the restaurant. I remember reading about Fritzel's in Kup's Column, but I don't remember going there.

Other than Marshall Field's, our other favorite department store was Carson Pirie Scott. We would go to Field's and Carson's, and our trips were always bookended with visits to both of those stores. I never understood why we did that each time, and I didn't enjoy shopping as much as other members of my family. However, one of my all-time favorite stores was Kroch's and Brentano's on Wabash, just north of Monroe, because you couldn't get books in Park Ridge except at a small bookstore that had a limited selection. I remember going to Kroch's and Brentano's every time I came downtown, and I insisted that we go there. When I began learning foreign languages in high school, if you went upstairs at Kroch's, there were books available in many languages. The selection of history books just seemed enormous. It was an expensive store to visit for me, but that was my idea of having fun in downtown Chicago.

As for museums, I would visit the Chicago Historical Society once in a while. When you grew up as a middle class kid in the suburbs at that time, even if your passion was history, the Chicago Historical Society wasn't the first museum you visited in the city. Besides, I really didn't understand the focus of the museum. The Chicago Public Library was much more a part of my life, and of course I learned a lot of history by studying art at the Art Institute of Chicago. Since then, I have met plenty of people my age that grew up around the Chicago Historical Society who formed a real attachment to it as their neighborhood museum.

By the time I was in seventh grade, I began coming downtown by myself or with friends. The best reason to come downtown was to do a paper for school. However, at that age, I didn't come downtown to hang out during the day or in the evening. Instead, I came to do something respectable and studious, but still used the time to roam around at my favorite places. I think of downtown now as being focused on North Michigan Avenue, while the original downtown I call the Loop.

The year is 1954, and a "blue goose" streetcar and several buses challenge autos for supremacy on State Street. John Wayne is featured in *The High and the Mighty* at the Chicago Theatre (courtesy of the Chicago Transit Authority).

A pair of southbound Chicago Motor Coach Co. buses arrive at Michigan and Washington in 1948. The main Chicago Public Library building is at left (courtesy of the Chicago Transit Authority).

Solutions to the problem of growing traffic congestion included converting several streets to one-way and designating lanes for exclusive use by public transportation. A recently-installed bus-only lane on Washington Street between State and Dearborn in April, 1957 (courtesy of the Chicago Transit Authority).

next page
The bus-only lane on Washington Street, looking west from the "L" at Wabash (courtesy of the Chicago Transit Authority)

James O'Connor

We went downtown regularly when I was growing up on the city's Southwest Side, and the biggest thing in our lives back then was to go to the Boulevard Room at the Hilton Hotel on Michigan Avenue for the ice show. That generally happened once a year. It was the Stevens Hotel at that time, but would become the Conrad Hilton. To the day she died in 1984, my mother could only refer to it as the Stevens, just like she called the Museum of Science and Industry the Rosenwald Museum.

The Empire Room at the Palmer House and the Chez Paree were nightclubs where Frank Sinatra and all the great entertainment names performed, but we never went there. Also, when I was growing up, we never went to jazz clubs.

When I was around 10 or 11 years old, I used to take music and judo lessons downtown. I was very young at that time, but I would get on the Illinois Central (IC) and come downtown by myself. Nobody gave any thought to it at that time. I would get on the streetcar at 79th Street, take it to the IC, ride downtown, and go over to Lyon and Healey on the northeast corner of Wabash and Jackson. Then, after my lessons, I would walk over, meet my dad, and we would drive home together. When I was 15, I was also an Andy Frain usher at downtown events, and, in high school, I worked on Friday nights on the docks of the *Chicago Tribune*. During all those years I wasn't driving, so it meant that I took the IC and the streetcar for my transportation. I went to St. Ignatius High School, and we used to hitch rides back and forth on Ashland from school each day. Everybody hitchhiked from my neighborhood and didn't think twice about it.

As for downtown, although I remember many of the restaurants where we ate, the only restaurant that seems to have been there forever is the Italian Village. There is the marvelous story that they tell about when Xerox was erecting its building at Dearborn and Monroe. They tried to buy the Italian Village and wanted to have the entire block become the Xerox building, but the family that owned the Italian Village said "no" to the first price, so they doubled it.

But again the family said "no," so Xerox added more money. Finally, the family told Xerox that there was no price at which they would sell the restaurant. It was where they had been since the 1920s, and that was where they were going to stay. That was one of the very few restaurants that has been very popular from the time it opened.

Of course, Henrici's and Berghoff's were popular destinations for people coming downtown. And Fritzel's was another landmark from that period. I also remember Shangri-La on State Street between Wacker and Lake. The big treat was to go to the Forum Cafeteria, which was on Monroe Street, and that was the best. The chains of restaurants that were so popular back then were O'Connell's and Toffenetti's, but O'Connell's had about a dozen locations scattered around the downtown area. They were great for roast beef sandwiches and fudge cake.

My family and I would come downtown about twice a year for movies, and we would often go to the Woods Theatre at Randolph and Dearborn because that was where they had the blockbuster openings for films like Bambi. In those years, it was a real treat to come downtown, and, of course, we would go to Marshall Field's during the Christmas season and sit under the tree in the Walnut Room. That really was a tradition in my family. Then, I watched as department stores like Sears, Wieboldt's, Goldblatt's, The Fair, and Stevens all closed. There used to be a wide variety of places to visit in the Loop, but we lost a lot of it as a greater percentage of the retail traffic seemed to be shifting to North Michigan Avenue.

The old East South Water Street entrance to the Illinois Central Suburban train station, with the Prudential Building rising in the background (Eric Bronsky Collection).

Randolph Street west of Dearborn in 1962 was dominated by the Woods Theatre, Greyhound Bus depot and the massive Sherman House Hotel. Note that Toffenetti had restaurants on both sides of the street (courtesy of the Chicago History Museum, ICHi-27848).

The Roosevelt Theatre stood directly across the street from Marshall Field's. Photographed in 1964, this movie palace was among the first buildings on "Block 37" to be demolished in the early eighties (photograph by Sigmund Osty, courtesy of the Chicago History Museum, ICHi-23907).

The ornate 1920s Palace Theatre on West Randolph Street was refitted to show Cinerama features in the fifties, and then Super Panavision 70 for *My Fair Lady* in 1964. Restored for live events, the venue is now known as the Cadillac Palace Theatre (courtesy of the Chicago History Museum, ICHi-35145).

J.J. Sedelmaier

Because I lived with my mom in Evanston and we didn't have a car until just before I graduated high school, we always went downtown on some form of public transportation, usually the "L." When I would see my dad on the weekends, we'd often venture into the Loop. Marshall Field's was frequently our destination. We'd get off the train and use the entrance that connected directly to the "L" platform. I'd hang out in the fourth floor toy department while my dad was visiting the book department.

We'd also go to movies at all the theatres—State-Lake, Woods, Michael Todd/Cinestage, Oriental, Chicago, etc. We'd also hit Wimpy's for lunch once in awhile. When I was young, my dad worked as an art director at advertising agencies and he once drew an ad for Wimpy's that was reproduced billboard-sized over one of their stores—very cool. He also designed the Northern Trust Bank logo (the one used for many years with the building over the type), so things like this bonded me with Chicago and the Loop.

Bookstores were another place that my dad and I would hang out. Krochs & Brentano's, under the "L" on Wabash, was terrific; we'd stay and browse for hours. They were the "BIG" bookstore in Chicago, and it's too bad they never grew like Borders and Barnes & Noble did.

We had relatives in New York and Ohio, and my mother preferred to travel by train, so this meant overnight trips to both destinations. Once again, the "L" came into play. Every Christmas, we'd take the New York Central to New York from LaSalle Street Station (which also had a direct connection from the Loop "L" platform), and, as we'd enter the terminal building, we'd pass the shoeshine chairs. To this day, the smell of cigars and the sound of Nat King Cole reminds me of this annual event. If we were going to Ohio, we'd take the Erie out of Dearborn Station.

When I was a young kid, we never had reasons to travel out of the B&O station (Grand Central), Union Station, or the IC station out on the lake. But when it was announced that these buildings were being closed and probably demolished, my dad took me to visit them. This definitely inspired my interest, respect, and passion for architectural preservation and restoration. Gawd, the Union Station concourse was gorgeous!

Sometimes, when going downtown on the "L", I'd see a train that fired up my imagination. It'd pull quickly and quietly into a station and then just as swiftly zip out. It didn't look like any other train on the "L" either in shape or color. It was blue/green with red stripes, and it had silver lightning bolts painted on the sides. My mom—further fueling the fantasy side of her son—said, "Oh, that's the "Mysterious Train." No one knows where it comes from or where it goes." A few years later I found out that it was the "Electroliner" of the Chicago North Shore & Milwaukee Railway that went from the Loop to Milwaukee; it discontinued service in early 1963.

By the time I entered high school, I was spending more and more time in Evanston, but after school in the fall and spring, probably when I should have been studying, I'd ride the "L" into the Loop. The trains at that time were from the 1920's, and you could open the windows fully. It was a beautiful ride. Most of the taller skyscrapers at one time or another had observation decks on their top floors. If you took the elevator to the top, you could usually find the remnants of the old public deck space and get a chance to see unique views of the city. I'd hang out in the Loop and take the Evanston Express back with the rush hour crowd.

Thinking back to what it must've been like a century ago, Chicago was a much different sort of place then because it was still forming itself. It had pulled itself out of the depths of destruction from the 1871 fire. It was a blank canvas, certainly from an architectural standpoint, and its personality was defined by the spirit necessary for its resurrection. Everything from the Depression to social reform has influenced its transition from a romanticized "City of Big Shoulders" to a cosmopolitan metropolis.

> "There is something about working downtown that gives you a swagger and makes you feel important, and gives an extra status to what you are doing."
> *Gary Johnson*

previous page
A prosperous State Street, looking north from the Van Buren "L" station in 1951 (photographer unknown).

The Chicago River, looking east from LaSalle Street in 1960. A new bridge was under construction at Dearborn Street (courtesy of the Chicago Transit Authority).

next page
This 1957 view looks north along the South Branch of the Chicago River from the Congress Expressway to the river's Main Branch. A transition is clearly underway. Wacker Drive and a brand new office tower along the riverbank are completed, but several of the old loft buildings remain. The old West Side "L" bridge was finally removed in the early sixties (Eric Bronsky Collection).

The Loop has acquired a patina that makes it feel warm and unique. Certainly the "L", in both appearance and sound, gives the downtown area a distinct personality. So many other cities have had to radically redo their downtown commercial areas, but Chicago's has evolved over time. Even though his methods may have often been questionable, Mayor Richard J. Daley was instrumental in protecting Chicago from going in the direction of some other large American cities. He was never going to let his hometown lose its identity, or deteriorate to the extent of a city like Detroit. The serpentine presence of the Chicago River and the open vista on Lake Michigan's shores also contribute to the overall picture.

One of Chicago's slogans is "The Second City." I can only assume that this refers to its status in relation to New York City. I've never understood why it's been necessary to diminish Chicago's reputation by resigning itself to a second position. I've lived in New York, I've worked in New York, and there's no comparing New York to any place on earth. The same holds true for Paris and I'm sure an endless list of other distinctive locations. Chicago has always been unique and continues to be so.

David Welch

I was born in Chicago, but I lived here only until I was 11 or 12. My parents are also native Chicagoans, but my grandparents came from England, Ireland, and Scotland. We were South Siders. My grandmother owned the building where we lived; we had the bottom apartment in the back, and she had the whole second floor. People say, "You can't remember streetcars, you're too young!" Well, we lived at 72nd and Wentworth, right there by the tracks, and you would hear this sound the streetcars made as they crossed over the South Chicago branch of the IC. Later on, buses replaced the streetcars.

My mother worked at Tribune Tower, just across the river from downtown. During my parents' generation, a lot more people worked downtown simply because that's where most of the jobs were; there weren't a whole lot of jobs in the suburbs back then. Everybody went to downtown Chicago. And State Street was the place to go.

After we left Chicago, my grandmother stayed on for five more years and I would come back to visit her a lot, so Chicago still had a pretty strong influence. My grandmother used to take me downtown a lot to go shopping. We'd go to Marshall Field's first, then she would hit the sales, and I remember going to another store—I believe it was Goldblatt's—where women were taking off their dresses and trying dresses on right out there in the aisles. I remember my grandmother towing me down there and in the basement there was a sale—I can picture it now, my grandmother was a very imposing woman over 6 feet tall—she would try on dresses and you would see her there in her big slip!

At Marshall Field's, we would eat under the tree in the Walnut Room, which in later years I took my daughter and granddaughters to, so that's three generations! Then we'd go outside and look at the windows. We always had fun there.

Downtown was a good place to go to in the early sixties, up until about 1965. That's when I parted company with the area, so to speak, for the military. But we would go downtown on weekends, and it was absolutely jammed with people! I'm not talking about the crowd going to the bars—it was families, adults, and couples. Rush Street really wasn't Rush Street yet, and Division Street had a few places, but it was not like downtown.

And, there were maybe a dozen movie theatres downtown. I went to the State-Lake Theatre and saw *The Dirty Dozen* six times ... with four different girls! The movie theatres in the suburbs were in the towns themselves; there were none yet in the shopping malls. We also used to go to the Avalon, where we would have Duncan yo-yo contests. And, at the Capitol on Saturdays, you could see 25 cartoons for a quarter.

At one time after I was married, I was a salesman and would call on drug stores like Walgreen's. Otherwise, going downtown was basically social and I never really worked there. My wife Babs (short for Barbara) and I were engaged Christmas of '67 in the Prudential Building, at the Top of the Rock; that's where I gave her the engagement ring. That used to be the place to go to if you wanted to see Chicago! In fact, my granddaughters were with us when we went to Millennium Park last summer. I pointed out the Prudential Building and said, "You know, kids, one day I'll take you all up there."

And, what a town! Even when State Street was no longer the street to go to, people still went there. I had opportunities to travel over a good portion of this country, and we have by far the nicest people in the country right here. If you need help, they're here for you. This mayor, I don't care what anybody says about him, he has done a wonderful job. He has made the town look absolutely beautiful. We go to Chicago every chance we get. I have friends who won't retire to the suburbs; they'd rather live in downtown Chicago.

A Designer Label Super Sale attracted a lively crowd of bargain hunters to the basement of Goldblatt's Department Store on March 19, 1981. As published in the *Chicago Sun-Times*. Photographer: Jim Klepitsch (Copyright 1981 by Chicago Sun-Times, Inc. Reprinted with permission).

following page
Fluorescent street lighting installed in the late fifties brightened an almost deserted State Street very late at night c. 1960 (Chicago Public Library, Special Collections and Preservation Division).

A Changing World

Downtown's problems were exacerbated by a duo of unexpected, unrelated, and tumultuous events during 1968. First, the Civil Rights movement and an increasingly tense racial situation culminated in riots that decimated Chicago's West Side following the assassination of Martin Luther King Jr. This was followed a few months later by the outbreak of violence in Grant Park at an anti-war protest during the Democratic National Convention.

What actually changed more than anything else was people's perception of Chicago. The migration of upper- and middle-class people away from the Loop had begun long before 1968 and was spurred by several sociological changes, not just racial. But, 1968 was surely a turning point. In the immediate aftermath of the turmoil, more people avoided downtown because they no longer felt safe there. Such a gut reaction was understandable for that time. Unfortunately, the city never fully overcame this stigma, and to the present day, many suburban residents remain uncomfortable about venturing downtown.

Perceiving the inner city environment as threatening or stressful—actually, this had much to do with traffic and congestion—families grew accustomed to a lifestyle that no longer revolved around going downtown. Outlying shopping malls, restaurants, and services were more accessible and offered free parking. Instead of going downtown to enjoy dinner at a good restaurant and see a movie, people chose to stay home and watch television.

Meanwhile, tens of thousands of commuters continued their daily trek to their jobs in downtown Chicago. But when 5 P.M. came, instead of lingering in the Loop to shop or dine, they would make a beeline for their cars, buses or trains. By 6 P.M. on weekdays and all day long on weekends, downtown streets were practically deserted.

Of course, such attrition took a devastating toll on retail businesses, especially restaurants that remained open during evening hours. By the early seventies, only a handful of Loop restaurants continued to serve dinner. If department stores fared better, it was only because their suburban branches were doing well enough to offset the waning performance of their State Street flagships, at least for a few more years. But many smaller stores, facing escalating rents and diminishing pedestrian traffic, either relocated away from the Loop or went out of business.

Economic development of predominantly African-American neighborhoods was virtually nonexistent. The selection of stores and entertainment venues in those parts of the city was meager at best, and the Loop beckoned because it was just a short bus or "L" ride away. Vacant storefronts along State Street were eventually rented to merchants who catered to African-American families. The ornate movie palaces, suffering from competition with television, were by then filthy and neglected. To survive, they switched their formats from first-run films to minority- and youth-oriented features.

Still, downtown hung on bravely due to private enterprise that invested heavily in redevelopment and new construction. Some areas including stretches of State, Randolph, and Van Buren Streets continued to stagnate, but elsewhere, new office towers began to rise at a frenetic pace. In fact, downtown commenced its first expansion into entirely new territory in 1969. An office and hotel tower development, known as Illinois Center (not to be confused with State of Illinois Center, and later renamed James R. Thompson Center) began to spring up east of Michigan Avenue. It was located between Randolph Street and the Chicago River on air rights directly above Illinois Central Railroad property. At the same time, the city extended the Wacker Drive viaduct east to Lake Shore Drive and also made improvements to the Randolph Street viaduct.

By the early seventies, downtown Chicago seemed destined to evolve into a sea of boxy office towers following the course of other major U.S. cities including Los Angeles, Houston, and Dallas. Service industries and white collar workers had replaced manufacturing and blue collar workers. Downtown thrived during regular business hours, but was mostly silent at other times. State Street's importance as a retail center continued to decline. One thing was certain though—more change was on the way.

"Richard J. Daley, being a very persuasive person, helped to keep downtown alive. If he wanted something, he could make things happen with the business community"
Jim McDonough

Mayor Richard J. Daley addresses a crowd of protestors at Civic Center Plaza in 1970. Originally published in the *Chicago Daily News*. Photographer: Charles Krejcsi (Copyright by Chicago Sun-Times, Inc. Reprinted with permission).

State Street looking north towards Randolph in the 70s
(courtesy of the Chicago Transit Authority).

This westbound sightseeing bus on Randolph at State is passing two
restaurants that once stood on what is known as "Block 37."
(Eric Bronsky Collection)

James McDonough

I worked for Richard J. Daley before he was elected mayor, when he was the Clerk of the Circuit Courts and I was at St. Ignatius High School. In my senior year, I ended up in the Marriage License Bureau signing licenses for Daley. Later, I was chosen by the mayor to be a supervisor on the Chicago Skyway, and then, in 1961, I was made the manager of the Skyway, which had opened in 1958. After being manager of the Skyway for a few years, in 1964, the mayor selected me as First Deputy Commissioner of Streets and Sanitation, the largest department in city government.

The snowstorm of 1967 was one of the most challenging assignments in my city career. Daley did a good job, and he was a great spokesman for the city, asking all Chicagoans to pitch in to help shovel out the snow. It became sort of a party atmosphere, as bad as it was. Soon, we got help from the state with their big plows. After the infamous snowstorm of 1967, I was appointed commissioner.

In 1968, when the Democratic National Convention was coming to Chicago, Mayor Richard J. Daley started with the idea of beautifying the downtown and the areas surrounding it. One time, I was driving with him and he said to me, "Come to my house tomorrow at 6:30 A.M." And, since it was special to be invited to his house in Bridgeport, I wanted to make certain that I wouldn't be late. I pulled up at his house and went in, and sure enough he was all dressed up. We drove around for probably two to three hours, going everywhere, and he spent all the time describing where he wanted places fixed and cleaned up around the city. We were coming back down Randolph when he saw some buildings that were dilapidated, so he said to me, "Jim, you've got to do something about those buildings"… and I wasn't building commissioner. I said to him, "Mr. Mayor. It will be done!" So, I got out of the car, went up to my office, and called Joe Fitzgerald (the building commissioner), and said to him, "Joe, I was just with the mayor and I was saying nice things about you. I want to inform you that I just agreed to take down three of those buildings on Randolph Street." He was upset because they were in litigation to remove those buildings. So I said to him, "Joe, I guess I will have to tell the mayor that you don't want to do it!" But, he did.

The biggest thing that I was involved in during the Richard J. Daley years was the infrastructure of the city, including Public Works and Streets and Sanitation. Although Richard M. Daley is known for the beautification of the city, it was his father, when he was the mayor, who started it all. During his administrations, he was upgrading the sidewalks and the greenery. His son gets credit for carrying the beautification of the city to a further degree.

As soon as the City finished paying off a seven-year loan for the lighting system along State Street, a group of civic leaders and State Street merchants gathered to symbolically burn the loan papers on September 22, 1965. As published in the *Chicago Sun-Times*. Photographer: Howard Lyon (Copyright 1965 by Chicago Sun-Times, Inc. Reprinted with permission).

Michael Demetrio

I was born on July 26, 1954 and grew up at Central Park and Grant in Evanston. Around 1950, my dad bought a large Spanish stucco house there for $32,000, and I never lived anyplace else until I went to college. I attended Evanston Township High School and then the University of Notre Dame, a place that every Demetrio went. After graduating from IIT Chicago College of Law with my law degree, I became a Cook County Assistant State's Attorney. My family moved to Lake County thinking that I couldn't follow them because it was outside Cook County, but I never had the heart to tell my father that I could have lived there. Instead of going north with them, I moved downtown.

While I was at Notre Dame, I met my future wife in 1972, and she is now a Circuit Court Judge. When I went to IIT, it was located, at the time, on the corner of Monroe and Wacker Drive. The building is not even there anymore. And, to show you how circular life is, I am teaching at the Chicago Kent College of Law in their beautiful new facility on Adams Street.

As for my earliest memories of downtown, they are focused on my dad. He was the owner-operator of not only Tynan's Restaurant on LaSalle Street, but he had a holding company through which he operated a number of different restaurants. His corporate headquarters was at 20 N. Wacker Drive in the Civic Opera House. I think that the reason for having his offices there was that he had a restaurant on the first floor called the Civic Opera Lounge. He did all the purveying for the Opera House and had an extremely large cafeteria that he operated in the building. His office was on the second floor, and there was a gigantic portico right outside his window. I actually remember when he would bring me downtown on Saturdays by car to do paperwork for his business I could literally crawl out of his office window and sit on the gigantic overhang of the building.

Among my earliest memories of State Street were the many movie theatres and Marshall Field's. We would go to Field's for special family trips. I was the youngest of four kids who included my brother Tom, my sister Cathy, and my oldest brother George "Ty" Jr., who was 14 years older than me and who was killed many years ago. We would come downtown every Christmas and eat lunch under the tree in the Walnut Room, and that was a wonderful tradition. I can remember a very bustling and busy State Street and not only Marshall Field's, but all the other large and small stores on that street.

When I was young and had started working for my dad at age 13, on special occasions when I was off from school, he would bring me downtown and we would go to a movie in the Loop. The very first movie I remember seeing with my father was *The Flight of the Phoenix* with Jimmy Stewart in 1966 that played at the beautiful and majestic Chicago Theatre. When I did start working in the restaurant and sometimes at the cafeteria, I was doing dishwashing in the kitchen, so there was no favoritism whatsoever. Later, I wanted to become a restaurant entrepreneur like Rich Melman, but that never happened.

While I was in college, my father moved his restaurant to Adams and Wells. The real estate firm, Hemsley Spear, had taken over the 1 North LaSalle building where Tynan's had been located, and that company decided they no longer wanted a restaurant in that building. So, they turned over the space to American National Bank and the bank was located there for many years. My father was at the end of his lease and decided to relocate his restaurant to 208 S. LaSalle, which is in the whole city block of LaSalle, Adams, Jackson, and Wells. That building is still there, but no restaurants are open in that building anymore.

There was an office manager from across the street at 134 S. LaSalle who used to eat at my dad's restaurant every day. The manager worked with my dad to get me a summer job as a janitor in that building, and I worked there for two or three summers as a member of Local 1, the Janitor's Union. This was in the 1970s, and in the summer between my junior and senior years at Notre Dame, I managed my father's restaurant and convinced him to take the summer off.

Across the street from our restaurant was King Arthur's Pub, which was owned and operated by Art Lieberman. Also, across Adams, there was a little restaurant owned by Bill Kotos. Bill had emigrated from Greece, and my father

mentored him in the restaurant business. When he came here, he couldn't speak a word of English and started out as a dishwasher. Then, he was a waiter at Berghoff's, and worked his way up until he owned this little place on Adams. Now, a McDonald's is located there, which is a sign of the times. My dad ended up selling Tynan's to Kotos, and the reason he sold the restaurant was because he didn't want me to take over the place and make my career there. He wanted me to become a lawyer like my older brother and someday work with my brother.

In fact, my older brother Tom, who works at Corboy and Demetrio, is the original Demetrio in the firm. One of Tynan's favorite customers was the legendary Judge James Geroulis. My dad was half Greek, but not with very much Greek influence because his father died when he was four or five years old and his mother had come to America from Dublin, Ireland. Her name was Catherine Tynan, and she became the genesis for the name of the restaurant.

I remember Tynan's, my dad's facilities on Wacker Drive, and how friendly he was with his competitors including Henry Bolling, who was older than my father. Bolling was an icon in the restaurant business, and his place was located at the south end of LaSalle Street by the Chicago Board of Trade. He had a number of restaurants, and his sons did carry on his tradition. Henry was a big, strapping man from Germany with a thick accent. I thought it was wonderful that within the restaurant industry there was competition, but that it was based on a high degree of civility and friendliness. Across the street from Tynan's was Johnny Lattner's restaurant, located near St. Peter's Church. My dad had been head football manager at Notre Dame for Elmer Leyden, one the "Four Horsemen." Thus, the Demetrios were really connected to the university and Lattner, who had been a star at Notre Dame, knew about my dad and looked up to him. Johnny was always asking dad for advice about operating a restaurant. Years later, Lattner's was destroyed in a gigantic fire.

St. Peter's Church is still located on Madison near LaSalle. I even remember going to confession there, and that was a part of many people's downtown life. My dad was downtown regularly during the week in those days because of the demanding business of operating restaurants—they were open for lunch and dinner—but he was always home on weekends because the restaurants were never open on weekends; there was never any weekend business. When we did come downtown on the weekends to do office work, LaSalle Street and any place west of State Street seemed to be relatively deserted.

So, looking back, I have been working downtown since I was 13 years of age; from being a busboy and dishwasher at dad's restaurant, working as a janitor on LaSalle Street during a couple of summers, going to law school after graduating from Notre Dame, working at the CBA Library, serving as president of Chicago Bar Association at 29 S. LaSalle, being a Cook County Assistant States Attorney, and, finally, having a partnership in my law firm of Corboy and Demetrio.

Downtown changed over the years in a way that was unfortunate because of the seeming demise of socialization among professionals … businessmen, stockbrokers, lawyers, and the people who worked in all the soaring skyscrapers. In the '50s and '60s, I think that people took a lot more time to interact with each other, and it usually revolved around eating or having a drink after work. Now, you just don't see it.

Another aspect of that era was people seemed to work harder and for longer hours. Back in those days, people wouldn't come down from their offices at the end of the day until 6 P.M. Then, they had a drink with their friends, and not just coworkers but other friends from all across the Loop. In those days, you didn't travel to Division Street or to the nightclubs to meet people. Guys would have their briefcase and newspaper as they came down from their offices, and they'd stop for a club soda or a Manhattan and spend more time socializing. I think that people were friendlier back then. Now, when you leave the office at 5 P.M., there is a mass exodus out of downtown towards their trains. So, when you walk along the downtown streets each day at 5:20 P.M., it has the feeling of being abandoned.

I don't think that the changing nature of the Loop impacted on the end of socialization. But what evolved was a new generation with different attitudes towards the after-work environment. The guys whom I remember so well were very successful lawyers, judges, and businessmen who put a great deal of value in personal relationships. I think that is what changed. The next generation that came through was much more college-educated. Back in the 1960s, a lot of the guys who were running big companies were guys who may have started in the company mailroom. That was how they rose to the top. I think what happened was, in the 1960s and 1970s, colleges and universities started putting so much emphasis on the value of technology and communications. Even today I don't get phone calls anymore. I get e-mails. I am the type of person who would much rather talk to someone and get something done instead of e-mailing back and forth.

When people started fleeing the Loop each evening, it seemed to lead to the demise of Loop centers like Tynan's or Gene Sage's. Sage had a place at One North LaSalle, too, and he and my dad were the best of friends. On Friday nights, I can remember that the Chicago police would set up blue "horses" outside Sage's so people could stand in line to go into the restaurant. It was a more personal relationship at that time between the businessmen and the police, and people enjoyed hanging out.

My dad stayed at Tynan's at Adams and Wells until 1976. But Sage's left the Loop. and King Arthur's Pub, which was a very popular place, went by the wayside. It was all because the customers weren't there anymore. I don't think that it was the move to suburbia that changed the Loop.It just became a fact that people decided it wasn't important to the professionals to talk to the guy in the next office or his customer over a drink or lunch. In fact, I remember when Mayor's Row was an icon and

where I learned more about law than I did sitting in the library on the fifth floor of the Daley Center. That happened because I was talking to very experienced lawyers. But, people began to leave the Loop at the end of the workday, and those important restaurants and bars no longer had the customers. So, they just decided to close.

State Street also changed for the same reasons. Along State Street and Wabash Avenue there were still these social centers where people would stop and shop before they decided to build the State Street Mall. The stores, restaurants, and theatres were open late in those days, and people stayed downtown in the evening. But, now, it seems that fast food places have replaced all the old restaurants. Back in the '60s, there were gorgeous theatres all over the Loop, but, even though some have been reopened, I look out from my window on the 21st floor and I still don't see the revival in terms of crowds and activity.

previous page
Tynan's bar was a popular after-work watering hole for lawyers and businessmen.

Tynan's owner George T. Demetrio is sitting in the restaurant's main dining room (both photos, courtesy of Michael Demetrio).

Mitch Markovitz

My earliest memories of downtown are my mom taking me to Marshall Field's on the Illinois Central. I remember Randolph Street Station before the Prudential Building was built, but what I really remember is eating in Field's Verandah, where they had tray meals. I would always get a hot dog, onion soup, and a cup of orange sherbet. It might sound awful, but I thought it was really great!

I remember getting on the 157 Ohio-Depot shuttle bus, the one that had the red flap on top that said 10¢ Shuttle, and going over to meet "Pop" at his studio in the evening after shopping. I vaguely recall streetcars downtown, but I have better memories of the variety of cars on the elevated besides the North Shore cars—like the wooden "L" cars with the gates, how noisy they were compared to all the other "L" cars. I always imagined that the center-door cars or any of the elevated cars with trolley poles went to some far-off and distant suburbs where life must have been better and the lawns were really green.

Around the time I started going to Northwestern Station, I became aware of the Madison Street bums. I remember one guy who kind of looked like Clark Kent; he said that he just lost his wallet, needed five bucks, and if I gave it to him he would put five dollars in an envelope and mail it to my father in a week. I gave him a raspberry!

I worked as an apprentice at my father's art studio during the summers of '65 and '66, and at Swan Studios in the Wrigley Building for a couple weeks during the summer of '67. I had to walk all over the Near North Side delivering packages for "Pop." Then, I worked downtown at Broadstreet's Men's Clothing from Thanksgiving of '67 until just after New Year's '68. My cousin and uncle both worked there. In fact, my uncle got me that job.

My interest in the South Shore Line started in 1952, when I was just two years old and noticed that their cars were orange. It was such a fascinating and unusual railroad that, bit by bit, my desire to work for them grew. Eventually, after stints as a trainman on the C&NW and Milwaukee Road,

I approached the South Shore's trainmaster…who wouldn't hire me because I wore glasses!

But I was still interested, and being proficient as a commercial illustrator I was inspired to start creating posters for the South Shore that emulated their famous advertising posters of the twenties. At that time, I was working as the art director for Deardorf Camera on the west side of the Loop. They still hand-made wooden view cameras—the typewriter at this place was so old the secretary had worn the letters off the keys. Venango River had just bought the South Shore Line from the C&O, and they had seen and become interested in my work. One thing led to another, and they hired me! I worked for them as art director, but then subsequent owner NICTD (Northern Indiana Commuter Transportation District) hired me as trainman and finally engineer!

What makes downtown unique? For being a big place, the Loop is really nicely contained and you feel cozy in it. It's like being in your own back yard, or knowing where all the bathrooms are in Marshall Field's—you don't have to think about it! I like the fact that you can look east and see a huge park and the lake. You might not necessarily see the water, but with no trees or mountains, you know there's a big open space.

I'm just sorry to see all the changes. Foreign cultures brought a lot of diversity to Chicago, but nowadays everything is homogenized. At one time, our society was a "sundae," but now we're a "milkshake." When it was a sundae, you could see all kinds of different textures, colors, and variances, but then we put it inside a blender to make a milkshake and it softened right up!

A modern South Shore Line train prepares to depart
Randolph Street Terminal several years before the 1926-era station
was rebuilt and covered over to facilitate construction of
Millennium Park (Eric Bronsky photo).

A CTA 10¢ shuttle bus heading east on Wacker Drive across
Dearborn in 1955 (courtesy of the Chicago Transit Authority).

George E. Kanary

Chicago kept on going as other big cities were dying. Downtown suffered because of outlying shopping centers...no question about it. The shopping centers were a little late to arrive around here, perhaps later than other cities. I remember when Lincoln Village, the first outlying shopping center in the area, opened in 1952. Then, in 1955, Lake Meadows Shopping Center opened up at 35th and South Park, now known as Martin Luther King Jr. Drive. These were new and modern, but neither had a major anchor store.

Change came slowly to downtown Chicago, but it did come. It seemed to follow the change in the city's demographics. In all, the momentum of having so many large department stores kept things going as long as it did. The Boston Store, as I recall, was the first store to close and that was in 1948. The theatre district stayed strong through the 1960s. That was an attraction that brought people downtown. The theatres continued after that, but then it became the "Kung Fu" film type of thing, and it discouraged a lot of people from going to downtown theatres.

A lot of the smaller shops closed or else moved out to the suburban shopping centers. Kranz's closed in 1947 and was replaced by a junk shop. Old Heidelberg became Tad's $1.09 Steaks, fried in the window—a greasy window, I might add.

It's a shame that the flagship State Street department stores have fallen, driven from business by the déclassé schlock operations of today. Generations of shoppers yet unborn will never know what a grand experience it was. The foolish arrogance of Macy's eliminating the world famous Marshall Field name amounts to crass stupidity! That beautiful store is now not doing well at all, and it may be lost. The shopping experience is a long way from what it once was.

The loss of the streetcars, particularly the ridiculous retirement of cars that were only six years old just to recycle their parts for building new "L" cars, was a hypothetical exercise in saving money. The $16,000 that was to be saved over the purchase of a new "L" car would buy a new propane bus. What they didn't consider is that the life of a propane bus was about one-third of the life of a streetcar, and the capacity of a bus was less than the capacity of a streetcar. So it was a bad deal overall, a sorry episode in Chicago's history.

The downtown circulator project would have been one of the better examples of government and private enterprise working together—the corporate taxpayers were willing to pay for it! At the outset, it was projected to handle 125,000 people a day just from the train stations. Typically, all the cities that have installed new light rail systems have exceeded their projected figures, often by double or even more. So, killing the circulator project was barbaric, in my opinion. One of the decided benefits of it was that it would have eliminated 350,000 bus trips across the Loop on an annual basis, certainly helping the clean air we all desire.

Chicago remains a tourist-oriented city. The Millennium Park project, even though it had large cost overruns, is a big attraction that's brought in lots and lots of people. Navy Pier is a fun place to go to, and the museums are as popular as ever despite the fact that they charge admission today. And, Chicago people are friendly to tourists. Oftentimes in the paper, you'll see a letter to the editor from people who maybe came with a jaundiced idea of what Chicago would be like, and once here, they just marveled at how friendly the people were.

Downtown Chicago now is like downtown Seattle; there's the old downtown, and there's a new downtown to the near north. Michigan Avenue shops are doing very well. I don't know that we would ever again see department stores built on the scale of Marshall Field's State Street store. What architect today would get away with designing those huge atriums, which are just lost sales space? And, all of the good places to eat are gone; we're left with the likes of McDonald's or Burger King. Where is an Elfman's sandwich shop when you need it?

Much of downtown's uniqueness was in the form of one-of-a-kind shops located in older buildings, where the rent was comparatively moderate. This one-block stretch of Madison Street between Franklin and Wells had a quirky bar called Ladner Brothers, a tiny eatery with sausages and onions grilling in the window, and fascinating stores such as All-Nation Hobby Shop (left) and Gemco Electronics, where one could spend an entire afternoon. This entire block fell to the wrecking ball in the late 1970s, replaced by glassy office towers (Eric Bronsky photo).

Clark & Barlow, located on the south side of Lake Street between LaSalle and Clark, was an old-world hardware store perhaps best known for its "Baldwin Flyer," a spring-loaded contraption that propelled money up to a cashier on a balcony overlooking the sales floor. This venerable store had to relocate when the entire block was cleared for Thompson Center (William C. Hoffman photo, Wien-Criss Archive).

Josephine Baskin Minow

While at Northwestern University, I met my future husband, Newton Minow. Years after our marriage, and with a broader perspective on life, I joined a group called "Focus" formed by Eleanor Peterson, a venturesome pioneer in race relations. We were seeking to ameliorate the racial tensions in Chicago. One of our goals was to integrate the staffs of those downtown department stores where hardly anyone of color was to be seen in the sales staff, in ads, the fashion shows, or as the window and floor models. Carson Pirie Scott was ahead of the pack, but the others were very slow to come around.

I was assigned to Marshall Field and Company, as well as to Saks on Michigan Avenue. Several of us made an appointment to see a senior manager at Field's, and I found it to be a memorably horrible encounter.

"You know, ladies, we've been here long before you and we will be here long after you, and Field's will not please our customers if we have black faces in our ads, fashion shows, window, or floor displays," he announced.

By the end of the conversation, he was so distraught his hands were shaking. He was very emotional. "You know, sir," I said to him, "Carson's is way ahead of you and has engaged people of color in many areas of their operation." He began to shake even more, his face reddened, and he dripped with perspiration.

However, that Christmas, to our surprise, Newt and I saw one decorated window at Field's where way in the back, if you looked closely, there was a little black chorus boy mannequin.

So, I said to Newt, "First the back of the bus, then the back of the window! Who knows what will happen next?"

The major physical change I remember about State Street was the construction of the Mall during the '70s. It was a wrong decision from the get-go, and I knew it right away. It became a major disaster for the Loop. Fortunately, the Mall is now a thing of the past, and traffic is once again allowed on State Street.

The worst decision, however, just took place in 2006, when the Macy name replaced the iconic Marshall Field and Company. Ironically, the brass plate with the Field's name has landmark status and can never leave the side of the building, but that is sad solace for those who grew up with the legendary store.

In essence, the downtown I knew as a youngster has been relocated to North Michigan Avenue and the Near North Side. The "State Street, that great street" of song, is no more.

Marshall Field's clock at the corner of State and Washington has always been a popular meeting place as well as the subject of a celebrated painting by Norman Rockwell. As published in the *Chicago Sun-Times*. Photographer: Nancy Stuenkel (Copyright 1989 by Chicago Sun-Times, Inc. Reprinted with permission).

The two Woolworth's stores on State Street were longtime Loop fixtures; in addition to the huge L-shaped main store between Washington and Madison, this edifice stood on the east side of State between Adams and Jackson. Both stores closed during the 1990s (courtesy of the Chicago History Museum, ICHi-30093).

Gary T. Johnson

The first time I had a serious job in the Loop was in 1970 after my sophomore year in college at Yale when I volunteered to work on the campaign to elect Adlai Stevenson III as U.S. senator. I came to work everyday just like it was a job, and, for the first time, I was commuting even though I wasn't getting paid. It was fun because I wrote position papers and briefing books in preparation for his suburban campaign presentations, and, once in a while, I wrote speeches for Adlai. It was a key event for me because I broadened my contacts and interests, and it looked good on my resume.

The Stevenson for Senator office was located above Hinky Dink's Bar on Clark Street just north of Madison on the west side of the street. We had big glass windows that faced east. It turns out that the U.S. Army under President Richard Nixon was spying on Adlai Stevenson from the Planters Hotel across the street, and they had cameras trained on us at the Stevenson Headquarters. The idea that they would bother spying on him was crazy.

There is something about working downtown that gives you a swagger and makes you feel important, and provides an extra status to what you are doing. So, that was the summer when I really got to know the Loop as someone who had made it my own as opposed to the occasional visit from the suburbs.

After I graduated from Yale, I was a Rhodes Scholar, went to Oxford, and spent two years getting an M.A. in English History. I was planning to go on to law school, but I loved studying history. Then I went to Harvard Law School and resolved to return to Chicago, have a family, and settle down in the mid to late 1970s. I didn't really see any changes in the downtown during those years even though, by then, the new First National Bank Building had been constructed. What I find astonishing is how long the hiatus was between the building boom that ended with the market crash and when the next skyscrapers were built in the Loop in the 1950s, such as the Prudential Building and the Inland Steel Building. I don't remember there not being the Prudential Building when I was growing up. I started practicing law in Chicago in 1977 at Mayer, Brown and Platt.

As for a changing downtown, I didn't see any dramatic changes by the late 1970s. But in 1979, Jane Byrne became mayor and I recall some changes to the Loop that are no longer here, which were sincere efforts to bring more dynamism to downtown. However, the State Street Mall had the opposite effect. It was based on forward-thinking European ideas about closing off streets to increase commerce and foot traffic. But Chicago, despite its dedication to public transportation, is still a big town for automobiles and has always been that type of city. As a result, it was a problematic venture to remove auto traffic from State Street.

I think that the Mall failed because it created a new "ghost town." People weren't ready to just walk up and down State Street. And buses with their constant exhausts were not where people wanted to hang out. People did whatever window shopping they were going to do anyway. It also meant that you could no longer drop a friend or family members off at Marshall Field's while you drove around in your car. You no longer had the kind of convenience that meant a lot to many people. And, the movie houses and theatres had closed by then or, if they were open, they weren't attracting people from the suburban neighborhoods. Around that time, North Michigan Avenue became a magnet and that was the place where people enjoyed walking.

In a funny way, I would say that my favorite time in Chicago history as it relates to downtown would be now. I'm not just saying it because I am president of the Chicago History Museum. I think that in terms of the growth and the changes that are occurring now, it is an exciting period. Millennium Park has pushed out the boundaries of downtown, although it remains to be seen whether the new park's popularity is going to spill over to the Art Institute, nearby museums, and downtown retail shopping. I think the concept of downtown as a growing residential center is very exciting.

Old post-fire buildings on Van Buren Street between State and Plymouth. These small buildings survived into the eighties. (Eric Bronsky photo).

The president of DePaul University has told me that apart from the University of Texas itself, Chicago is now the biggest conglomeration of students in the country because of all the dormitories that have been developed across downtown. The idea that these old stores are being reused for residential housing and student life is very exciting. I think that the consequences are going to spill through the Loop with the opening of more bookstores, small stores, and coffeehouses. This will mean that there are places to hang out, and there will be lots of life in the Loop at night. It is different from when I was a lawyer downtown because then, when darkness fell, people fled the downtown area and there was no one on the streets.

Our downtown is unique from other cities because of the idea that someone has drawn a circle called the Loop. In New York, there are subways that go through, but in Chicago, there is actually a loop, and there used to be an "L" route known as the Loop Shuttle that would make a circle trip around this defined area. There is a compactness that you don't have in other major American cities, and the closeness is important. People usually walk in the Loop rather than taking a cab, and there are very few downtowns where you can do that. You are considered to be some sort of wimp if you take a cab, even if it is a seven or eight block walk.

As for the city's image of toughness, you have to start with the fact that the stockyards had a major impact on the city. If you were downtown or on the South Side and the wind blew from the southwest, you could always smell the stockyards. I think that when that smell was no longer there it tangibly changed the nature of the Loop and sort of civilized the experience of being downtown. When you move forward to the transformation of the Loop with the introduction of Starbucks and the yuppies, the whole nature of downtown changed. I think that the reason why the Starbucks phenomenon was possible was that the Loop was always a walking place. In other cities, people would always drive to where they were going and they would pull into garages in the building where they needed to be. But downtown Chicago always had little places you could go to because people always were walking from place to place. I always found the most interesting places in the Loop located on the streets where the "L" was built. I think those were less desirable in real estate terms. So, those were the buildings that were torn down the latest, like the little places on Lake and Van Buren. The continuing existence of the walking trade meant that the Starbucks phenomenon could occur.

If I could change one aspect about the current downtown, I would bring back the streetcars, even though I barely remember them. The cities that have kept their streetcars are happy that they did it. I think that if there had been streetcars down State Street rather than buses, they wouldn't have had to feel the need to create a mall back in the 1980s.

Bernard Judge

After college, in the '60s, the Blue Note had closed, so we moved to Rush Street for entertainment and never came back downtown. Television, not racial change, had "knocked" all of the big theatres out of business. By then, downtown had very little going on at night, and, after dark, it seemed that the Loop became abandoned. I remember that after I got married in 1966, we went downtown to see the movie *Clockwork Orange* at the Michael Todd Theatre on Dearborn.

The Chicago Police were just beginning to wear their portable radios by that time, and in the movie, society was changing, urban decay was occurring, and there was an increase in violence. Even though the movie took place in the future in London, there were a lot of parallels to Chicago of those years.

That night, three guys were sitting in front of us in the show smoking marijuana and cheering the violence in the movie. My wife was pregnant, and the situation was very intimidating. We left the theatre when the movie ended and went to get our car in a parking garage across the street. There was a "Superfly" character in the garage screaming at the manager because somebody had scraped the side of his car. The cops with the crackly radios were there, and the whole scene was so intimidating that I said to my wife we would never come downtown again. And, I didn't bring her there again for years because it felt so unsafe.

By the '70s, it was no longer very pleasant to go downtown, even if you worked there. All the regional shopping centers had opened by those years, so you didn't have to shop in the Loop. Then, during the mall years when they closed off State Street to traffic (except for buses), down-town was almost empty after the end of the work day. The State Street Council and probably Mayor Jane Byrne wanted the mall, hoping it would keep people downtown. Since they weren't getting people to come downtown with State Street being open to traffic, they decided to try the mall approach. But then they never really made it into a mall because they decided to let the CTA run its buses on State, making the outside mall unpleasant. And, retail was getting shoddier along with the steady concentration of buses on State Street.

It wasn't relaxing to be there, and it never, ever had a chance to be successful. However, Marshall Field's remained the icon on State Street, especially during Christmas. I remember that I bought all my suits at Field's after the holidays when they went on sale for unbelievable discount prices.

As for legitimate theatre, we would go downtown to a play once, twice, or three times a year. You could go to the Schubert or the Blackstone Theatres, and they would have decent plays, even if they had second level casts.

In the early part of the '60s, I was a jazz fan and the jazz in Chicago was second to none in terms of stars and quality. For example, we went to the Sutherland Hotel on 47th and Drexel, and the Maryland Hotel; and there were these small bars that offered great jazz, like the Lake Meadows Bar where Ramsey Lewis began his career, and Al Hibler would sing there often. There were a half a dozen places that you could go to on the Near North Side, like the Plugged Nickel in Old Town, where they had the very best jazz musicians. We would go to Mister Kelly's where you didn't have to have dinner, but could just sit at the bar and nurse two drinks to hear one set. The London House was open in those years, and you could see great entertainment there all the time. The Marienthal Brothers finally closed both places because they probably tired of operating the clubs.

However, it is amazing how downtown has made a great comeback. Today, we have a much bigger upper middle class that has opted to move downtown from the suburbs. They want to go to the cultural events and eat at fine restaurants. Now, there is so much to do downtown that you don't have the time to really do a lot of it…but it's nice to know that you can.

Despite the rise of television and a steady decline in attendance, the Blackstone Theatre on East Balbo Drive was among a handful of legitimate theatres that managed to survive until the South Loop's renaissance got underway. This venue, currently owned by DePaul University, is now the Merle Reskin Theatre. The Pancake House was flattened (courtesy of the Chicago History Museum, ICHi-20853).

The State Lake Theatre on a very quiet Sunday in 1980. As published in the *Chicago Sun-Times*. Photographer: Carmen Reporto (Copyright 1980 by Chicago Sun-Times, Inc. Reprinted with permission).

James O'Connor

After college and graduate school, I returned to Chicago and began my career at Commonwealth Edison. During the '60s and '70s, downtown was a pretty barren place after 5:30 or 6:00 P.M. I think it happened when the restaurants began to close and there weren't as many places that people had enjoyed in the past. It was no longer as fashionable to come downtown, and there were clearly some tensions in the city during the '60s and '70s that reflected the city's racial changes. I don't think that people adapted to those changes as well as they could have at that point, and there was obviously an increased level of fear that was reflected in the downtown environment.

I think that in reality, the riots of the 1960s on the West Side, along with the deteriorating quality of the housing stock, and the abandonment of the close-in neighborhoods by tradition-al ethnic groups—where you had some areas that were almost exclusively Polish, Irish, German, Italian, and Jewish—all affected downtown and the areas around it. You just had a lot of different groups that were fortified by restaurants, shopping, and religious institutions that promoted the allegiance to the ethnic group that they represented. As those began to disintegrate over time and people left out of fear, quality of education, or the perception that the neighborhoods were deteriorating, the basic fabric was ruptured. And those changes had an impact on downtown because the neighborhoods were no longer adjacent or near to downtown on the other sides of the expressways.

Anyway, the big thing about Commonwealth Edison and downtown Chicago was the discussion during the 1970s of the idea that the Loop "L" should be torn down and placed underground. The main reasons given were that the "L" was loud and squeaky, people felt that the steel girders detracted from the appearance of the Loop, and the elevated structure represented a boundary that you didn't go beyond. There was an awful lot of emotion about whether to tear down the Loop "L" until they looked at what it would actually cost to replace the structure. In the case of Commonwealth Edison, we had hundreds of millions of dollars worth of facilities involved if they had to take down the "L" structures. If they had to remove the Commonwealth Edison facilities, it would have resulted in a huge amount of movement of utility facilities along with a potential disruption of service for downtown buildings. A lot of thought was given to it, along with serious economic analysis.

There were modernization programs going on in cities around the world where utilities were being placed underground rather than building overhead systems. The feeling in Chicago was that such a change would make downtown more attractive, and it would be a continuous downtown instead of one that was punctuated by the "L" that surrounded it. But as time wore on, a lot of people began to think of the Loop "L" structure as a city landmark. It so identified Chicago that if you removed it, and even though it might have helped to beautify things, we would have lost a major element of what made Chicago different from any other major city. It also defined the term "Loop." So, I think that after a while, when people had a chance to look at the costs of such a change and the potential for disruption, it was decided that there were other priorities that needed to be addressed in the city and we could live with the Loop "L". Of course, the sound of the elevated as it went around corner tracks was a major part of the

following page
The Loop "L" structure was imperiled for many decades before
Chicagoans finally began to appreciate its historical significance and view
its lacy ironwork as a dynamic symbol of Chicago's muscular resolve
(Eric Bronsky photo).

discussion. But they finally dropped the idea although the push for a change had some real traction for a while. Even though I was only a vice president at Com Ed and not in the senior executive ranks during those years, we were providing a lot of data as to what the economic consequences would be. One example was the discussion about removing the substation in the middle of the Loop on Dearborn Street in what is now known as Block 37. That is the electric nerve center for the whole downtown area, and there was a suggestion that the city could do a lot of things in terms of putting up new buildings there if Com Ed could get rid of the substation. But, then the question became—where would you put the substation? No matter where you put it, it had to be partly above ground because of cooling requirements and it would be costly to relocate the substation.

I remember Arthur Rubloff saying to me, "If you could get rid of that substation it would really make everybody's life a lot easier." My response was, "Arthur, where would we put it? Where do you want it to go so it's not going to be a problem? We can't put it too far away as a major power source for downtown buildings." And the economics of any relocation were huge, so that idea was eventually dropped. But for several years, every time a developer would come along they would say, "If you can rid of that, we can build a mega-building on that site." We always felt a little guilty that it was blocking a major development. But at the same time, we recognized that if it wasn't there, it would have to go somewhere else that people would have found undesirable. We had all sorts of schematics presented to us that suggested that if we couldn't relocate it, then someone could build around it, over it, or disguise it. Yet, we still needed access, and we were worried that something might fall on top of it. And now they are building around it at Block 37 rather than removing it.

My reaction to the State Street Mall is that it was well-intentioned. And yet it never worked because it didn't have the desired free flow of pedestrian traffic. At that period of time, the Loop was suffering because of the rise of North Michigan Avenue and the Golden Mile. A lot of the retailers who had significant investments, such as Marshall Field's, opened new stores on Michigan Avenue or built new ones. That seemed to be a more desirable shopping area because there was a better concentration of the key retail names than they had if they just continued to stay downtown. The State Street Mall never captured the imagination of people, and it wasn't a destination as some people hoped it would be, unlike Millennium Park, which has really become a major destination. The park has moved the center of gravity of the city further south and has taken away some of the focus from North Michigan Avenue.

Paul Meincke

I arrived in Chicago in 1985 to work for WLS-TV. However, the first time my family came to Chicago was in 1963 when we took the Rock Island Line from Rock Island, Illinois, my home town, to see a White Sox doubleheader. When we went to Comiskey Park in '63 for the ballgame, I remember walking behind the old scoreboard and just looking back at the city and marveling at the skyline. It was a doubleheader, and the first game lasted 18 innings while the second game went 23 innings. We didn't get home until 4:30 A.M. We were supposed to visit the original McCormick Place on the lake to have dinner, but we didn't get there until midnight.

That trip was my first exposure to skyscrapers, and I remember that when we got off the train at LaSalle Street station, we walked along State Street and saw all the hustle and bustle. Even at the age of 13 years old, I tried not to act like a tourist, but I was still looking up at those magnificent buildings. I had an overwhelming reaction to the city because of the great energy and it became a "wow" experience. I graduated from high school in 1968, and part of the treat was to come to Chicago to see a Cubs game at Wrigley Field and go to the Prudential Building which was, at that time, the tallest building in Chicago. It was like I was in the stratosphere when we were at the top of that building, but of course, the Prudential Building is now dwarfed by so many other taller buildings.

When I came to Chicago in July 1985 from a television job in Cleveland where I had been for four years, I didn't really know anybody in the city since my in-laws lived out in Barrington. I was staying downtown at the Sinclair Hotel. One night, I didn't have anything to do, so I went over to the Woods Theatre on Dearborn and Randolph and discovered what a "rat trap" it was. I didn't realize it at the time, but people said to me, "You went there to see a movie? Don't you know that there are rodents living there?" The movie was *Mad Max Beyond Thunderdome*. I had some popcorn, and my shoes were sticking to the floor. That movie theatre is long gone, and Block 37 was here when I arrived in Chicago. Everything hadn't been torn down on that block, and there were some lower level buildings still standing, facing across State Street to Marshall Field's.

In 1985, I was struck by the unevenness of State Street. The Mall's pedestrian walkway was very wide, and there was only two-lane traffic on the street. Later, State Street was widened and reopened to auto traffic, and the sidewalks were pushed back to where they are today. Channel 7 was under construction—seemingly forever—at that time. The studios were at 190 N. State Street on the twelfth floor, and the newsroom was on the ninth floor. The State-Lake Theatre was gone by then, and what they had done was to build the current building inside the old theatre building. If you were to peel off the current ceiling tiles at Channel 7 today, you would find the old projection booth for the State-Lake Theatre out there in the middle of the newsroom.

By the 1980s, a downtown that I had remembered as being very vibrant had begun to include a lot of seedy-looking shops and beat-up looking places on State Street. You would turn a corner and find buildings in horrible disrepair. But a lot of that has changed now, and by the early 1990s, downtown became much different. I remember the Leo Burnett Building going up and the Renaissance Hotel on State and Wacker. There is a new parking lot on Lake and Dearborn that replaced a small, ramshackle-looking parking lot, and physically it's more aesthetic and presentable.

The Chicago Theatre was closed and kind of beat-up looking for a while, but they brought it back as a grand entertainment venue. I had no idea that the Oriental Theatre was still there, and it has now been returned to all its previous grandeur. Then, the plays were brought back on a regular basis and the Theatre District made a comeback. I'm anxious to see what they do with the supposed alley behind there that will run from State to Dearborn. I don't know if that is going to happen, but it is supposed to become a walkway between the Goodman Theatre and the Chicago Theatre so that there is a direct connection with the developing Theatre District. The first time I went into the newly refurbished Oriental Theatre, I was blown away. It has captured this great sense of Chicago history, and that is the same thing with the Chicago Theatre.

Chicago has done a good job of making its buildings "welcoming" since they are not built right up to the street. It is also true of the Beitler Building where Montgomery Ward's used to be on South State Street. That's a change because it was an empty lot forever. The Harold Washington Library is another big change.

State Street is a lot busier now with people moving about at varying late hours. I suppose that I feel safer now because when I first started at WLS-TV and would walk to the train, I would make a turn on darkened Lake Street and run into some strange individuals. I now come into the city from Des Plaines, get off at the Thompson Center, and walk to the studios from there. With the development of the Theatre District, and more importantly because more people are living downtown, there has been a huge population explosion, including the college dorms that are located near the studios. So, you get to see and interact with people of all ages, colors, interests, and costumes, which have helped to create a sense of vibrancy downtown. As a result, downtown is much more reassuring and comfortable. Those changes bode well for the future.

The projections for the next 20 years show a population of 400,000-500,000 living downtown, including the new Millennium Building that will have views of Grant Park and condos and penthouses costing $3 million plus. That means a lot of people will be living in and around the Loop, and in addition to all of the conversions, new spires are going up from the south to the north end of downtown. There certainly has been a lot of rehabbing of older buildings that would have otherwise "died" or given way to something else. Such redevelopment surely extends to the near West Side, which was quite seedy when I arrived in 1985. The WLS garage was located on West Madison in Skid Row, and that was where we kept our trucks. It was a scary place, but now the 9-1-1 Center is over there, and the Palace Grill is right across the street.

When I come downtown and walk around anytime of day or night, I feel safe and it's a nice feeling. However, many suburbanites still don't have that sense of safety. And, if the downtown not been given proper guidance and money to invest, the whole downtown could have failed. Mayor Richard M. Daley has been the key actor in making it happen.

It is also fascinating to walk up and down Wabash Avenue. I remember that my aunt and uncle, who lived in Princeton, Illinois, used to tell me how they would love to visit Chicago, go to Berghoff's, and then to Rose Records to buy records. When I got to Chicago, I was walking and exploring downtown because I thought that the best way to learn the town was to walk the Loop and ride the "L" everywhere. I was in Rose Records, and I thought that it was a great experience. I continue to discover walkways under the Loop that run from building to building...pedways that run under the streets. There was once a whole freight railway system under downtown, but later with the flood, we demonstrated the vulnerability of the city.

PART IV
LOOP RENAISSANCE
1980s-2000s

Loop Renaissance

Downtown Chicago managed to survive and thrive through a critical period when the central business districts of other northern industrial cities, including Detroit and Cleveland, were in decline. To understand the factors that steered Chicago on a steadier course, we must turn the clock back to 1955, the year Richard J. Daley was elected Mayor.

Daley loved downtown and Daniel Burnham's legacy. To his credit, he was a remarkably strong politician who personified the parochial and resilient nature of Chicagoans. He was skilled at obtaining federal and state monies to fund major civic projects, and he had a knack for luring businesses and economic development to the city's center, key factors that propelled the building boom and kept the Loop humming. Years before environmental concerns became a mainstream objective, he publicly expressed his dream that one day it would again be possible to go fishing in a cleaned-up Chicago River.

Over the long run, not everything the Daley administration did worked for the betterment of downtown. He was not an advocate of historic preservation, and one venerated Loop landmark after another crumbled during his watch. Pushcart vendors, street musicians, and sidewalk cafes, which enhanced street life in New York and elsewhere, were less than welcome here. The intent to improve mass transit and enhance traffic flow by replacing streetcars with buses was a tragic misstep. There was also a plan to build additional subways that would permit the Loop "L" to be torn down, but this grew into a costly boondoggle that never got past the drawing board. And while Daley knew was adept at stimulating economic development and growth, it was a greater challenge to stem the tide of individuals and families who were drifting away from the city and especially its downtown.

The revamping of State Street into a transit mall, conceived during the Daley years and finally begun in the late seventies by his successor Michael A. Bilandic, was intended to curb attrition and boost retail business. Unfortunately, retail stores pinning their hopes to a turnaround that never came gradually abandoned State Street.

Department and other significant stores that shut down during the eighties included Charles A. Stevens, Wieboldt's, Maurice Rothschild, Goldblatt's, Montgomery Ward, Lytton's, Bond, and the original Sears. By 1990, only two traditional department stores remained in the Loop—Field's and Carson's—and business at these two locations was marginal at best. Rather than invest substantial capital towards updating their State Street flagship, the Field family got out of the department store business altogether, selling their stores to a British tobacco conglomerate in 1982.

The failure of the mall was in part attributable to the continued erosion of retail business and the unwillingness of new developers or retailers to invest. The block directly across the street from Marshall Field's, known as "Block 37," had become especially seedy and blighted. In anticipation of a major commercial redevelopment, all of the buildings on that block were leveled in the early eighties, but then, due to economic instability and political squabbling, Block 37 remained empty for over two decades. Steelwork for a multi-use commercial development finally began to rise during 2006.

Other projects initiated during the Bilandic years to bring people back downtown proved more successful. The public's enthusiasm for the first ChicagoFest at Navy Pier in 1978 spurred other seasonal events and led to capital improvements to the Pier. Well-publicized cultural events flourished in Grant Park and other nearby public venues. CTA's Sunday "Culture Bus" service offered scheduled departures from the Art Institute, ferrying Chicagoans and tourists to cultural and historic attractions in and around downtown. Such activities attracted visitors to Chicago where they, of course, patronized Loop hotels, stores, and restaurants.

Mayor Jane Byrne's term during the early eighties ushered in a decade of political rivalry in City Hall, but reviving downtown was high on her list of priorities. Taste of Chicago was launched in 1980, and the two-week-long Loop Alive! Festival during February brought people downtown for cultural attractions, entertainment, and retail promotions at a traditionally slow time of the year. Her successors, Harold Washington and Eugene Sawyer, focused more on problems in the neighborhoods but maintained the status quo (an exception was ChicagoFest, which had been losing money). The updating of ordinances to permit licensing of street vendors, musicians, and sidewalk cafés in the Loop area breathed some new life into downtown streets.

During the eighties, Chicago's architecture heralded the postmodern era with radical departures from the austere and monolithic boxes of the sixties and seventies. Notable works included Helmut Jahn's James R. Thompson Center and Philip Johnson's 190 South LaSalle tower, whose gabled roofline emulated a long-gone Loop landmark, the Masonic Temple. By then, urban planners and architects had become attuned to the need for pedestrian-friendly spaces. Outdoor plazas received makeovers and began to host special events. Several buildings with usable retail space below street level were conjoined with a network of passageways into the all-weather pedway extending from the LaSalle Street entrance of City Hall to the Prudential Building east of Michigan Avenue.

Also during the eighties, two significant trends merged to become an important component of downtown Chicago's rejuvenation. The first was the growing historic preservation movement. The National Historic Preservation Act of 1966 and the Commission on Chicago Landmarks, established in 1968, paved the way to protection for several architecturally and historically significant buildings in the Loop.
The exteriors and interiors of some of Chicago's more prominent skyscrapers were cleaned and restored. Ironically, the Loop "L," for many decades despised and derided as a barrier to commercial development, became a respected icon. Its steel structure was refurbished, and the station at Quincy and Wells was restored to its original appearance. Restoration of the Chicago Theatre to its original opulence in 1986 led to other extant Loop theatres receiving the same treatment.

The second trend was adaptive reuse. The dowdy main Chicago Public Library building, which Richard J. Daley fully intended to demolish until his wife Eleanor put her foot down, was refurbished into the sparkling Chicago Cultural Center. Dearborn Street Station, empty and derelict after 1971, was rehabilitated into commercial space in the mid-eighties. Buildings that formerly housed department stores became college campuses with smaller retail stores fronting State Street. The shabby Reliance Building, its classic Chicago Style façade long desecrated by a gaudy neon sign for Karoll's Men's Wear, became the Hotel Burnham.

The Daley dynasty returned to City Hall in 1989 with Mayor Richard M. Daley restoring many of his father's values and priorities that had spurred downtown development during the 1955-1976 time period. He aspired to reverse the attrition of people and retail business from downtown, and attract more tourism and convention business to Chicago. Revival of the long-neglected South Loop had been underway several years before the second Daley took office. Following the construction of the Dearborn Park residences, redevelopment of the Printer's Row district along South

"I remember that before it was built I had mental images of a beautiful street being converted into a beautiful, park-like mall. And, when they finished it, I remember looking at the mall and thinking, 'Is this all there is?'"
Potter Palmer IV

Dearborn, and completion of the Harold Washington Library in 1991, the once dilapidated area became fashionable as people sought to occupy newly converted loft residences or open upscale restaurants. The success of this dramatic turnaround spurred rejuvenation of the North Loop and particularly the Theatre District, focusing on the State and Randolph intersection and radiating outward.

Downtown streets themselves had to be improved by the city in order to stimulate further economic development through private investment. State Street Mall's 1996 makeover into a more inviting thoroughfare and its reopening to auto traffic was an expensive gamble that slowly began to reverse the street's decline. The return of a Sears department store to State Street in 2000, remarkably in the same building that had once housed The Boston Store, renewed optimism for that street's comeback as a retail center. Michigan Avenue and LaSalle Street were subsequently improved with boulevard-style landscaped medians. Wacker Drive was completely rebuilt with its historic character not only intact but enhanced. Other major streets received replicas of ornate old style cast iron light poles, which replaced the ubiquitous mercury vapor light poles of the '50s and '60s.

But, over the course of several decades, retail business continued to bifurcate into two distinctly separate zones. The newer retail tenants along State and Wabash reflect the transition from locally owned stores serving the middle and upper classes to value-oriented national chains aimed towards students, minorities, and the working class. Nearly all of the more exclusive and upscale stores that cater to tourists and the elite preferred the newer and more fashionable retail "downtown" strip along North Michigan Avenue between the Chicago River and Oak Street. So, the Loop's traditional shopping district had evolved into a decidedly different flavor than in the past.

While these changes were taking place, a building boom of a different sort was slowly gaining momentum. This was not a commercial but rather a residential boom. Beginning with Marina City in 1964, construction of apartment and condominium towers had continued sporadically for two decades on the outer fringes of the Loop. The Loop itself was not zoned for residential use. However, this changed with an overhaul of the zoning ordinance to permit the construction of new condominium towers and the adaptive reuse of existing commercial structures as residences.

The year 2000 was a turning point for downtown Chicago in several respects. Redevelopment of the blighted northwest corner of State and Randolph with a postmodern residential tower for the School of the Art Institute began a new transition—evolution of the Loop itself into a residential neighborhood. Condominium projects were soon underway nearby, and neighborhood-type retail businesses like hardware and grocery stores eventually began to contemplate locations along State Street and Wabash Avenue. Brand new hotel towers rose, and more traditional hostelries, like the legendary Palmer House Hilton, were extensively refurbished or restored.

Working from architectural drawings by designer Kiyoshi Kikuchi, Eric Bronsky built this conceptualized scale model of State Street Mall as a design tool for the City of Chicago Bureau of Architecture during 1977 (Eric Bronsky photo).

But downtown's most dramatic success story of recent years is what took place east of Michigan Avenue. The rebuilding of the Lake Shore Drive S-curve, the makeover of Navy Pier, the creation of a museum "campus" and ultimately the completion of Millennium Park signify a collective fulfillment of the dreams of many Chicago leaders, past and present, with a vision for the city's future. Where once stood an unsightly expanse of railroad yards, parking lots, and warehouses is now a fully developed mixed-use extension of the central city that includes well-planned access and, just as important, open space.

So, the first decade of the twenty first century saw downtown Chicago basking in one of the most prosperous eras in its history, and yet there remained a palpable brittleness. The city's problems, not the least of which was public transportation, were far from solved. September 11, 2001 changed downtown by enhancing our awareness of its vulnerability, making security a much higher priority than it had ever been. And economic development in the Loop continued to ride with the peaks and valleys of the nation's economy.

Cities are transient places where nothing stays the same for very long. Businesses will continue to come and go. Sociological trends are constantly on the move. Sooner or later, a new mayor might have a different set of priorities. A lot can change...and inevitably, it will.

The groundbreaking ceremony for State Street Mall took place on June 17, 1978 at the intersection of State and Randolph. Mayor Michael A. Bilandic and State Street Council Chairman and Marshall Field & Co. Executive Vice President Arthur E. Osborne wielded symbolic jackhammers for press photographers. As published in the *Chicago Sun-Times*. Photographer: Perry C. Riddle (Copyright 1978 by Chicago Sun-Times, Inc. Reprinted with permission).

The west side of State Street, looking south from Washington during construction of the Mall c. 1979. Furnishings included kiosks, planter rings, and shelters over bus stops and subway entrances (Chicago Public Library, Special Collections and Preservation Division).

Wieboldt's flagship department store, located in the former Mandel Brothers' building at State and Madison, invested in a complete interior renovation during the mid-70s. Here, hostess Ruth Brown welcomes a shopper to the "new" Fashion First Floor. Originally published in the *Chicago Daily News*. Photographer: Charles Krejcsi (Copyright 1976 by Chicago Sun-Times, Inc. Reprinted with permission).

A rebuilt subway entrance on the west side of State Street, looking south towards Madison. Wieboldt's "modernized" edifice is visible at left. That store's sales continued to decline after the Mall's completion and it eventually closed. Today, T.J. Maxx and Filene's Basement occupy part of the former Wieboldt's space, and the building's exterior has been restored to its original appearance (Chicago Public Library, Special Collections and Preservation Division).

All Loop department stores were looking for ways to stimulate business. Marshall Field's now defunct Crystal Palace Ice Cream Parlor was a popular destination, even during cold weather. As published in the *Chicago Sun-Times*. Photographer: Howard Lyon (Copyright 1975 by Chicago Sun-Times, Inc. Reprinted with permission).

A group that possibly includes State Street Council members inspects the Mall c. 1981. At nights and on weekends, when there were relatively few buses, State Street was nearly deserted (Chicago Public Library, Special Collections and Preservation Division).

"Louis on the Mall" was operated by Carson's in front of their State Street store during the summer of 1982, following legislation to permit sidewalk cafés and pushcart vendors on State Street (Chicago Public Library, Special Collections and Preservation Division).

next page
The west side of State Street, looking south from the Lake Street "L" in 1993. The construction barricades surrounding Block 37 had been up for a decade and restoration of the Reliance Building (background) as the Hotel Burnham had not yet commenced. As published in the *Chicago Sun-Times*. Photographer: Ellen Domke (Copyright 1993 by Chicago Sun-Times, Inc. Reprinted with permission).

Jerome R. Butler

I grew up in Chicago's Edgewater area. Some of my earliest recollections of downtown include going to one of the ice cream parlors on State Street and visiting Marshall Field's with my mother and sister before Christmas. I also recall trips with my father in the thirties to look at bridges under construction along the Chicago River and occasional visits to the Navy Pier area to buy smoked fish.

My father was Bridge Engineer for the city of Chicago. He was responsible for the design of numerous bridges and viaducts, including Wacker Drive, and he also had quite a few friends who were architects. I think it was because of my father's influence more than anything else that I decided to pursue a career in architecture.

In 1947 I became a student at the University of Illinois branch at Navy Pier and spent three years at their School of Architecture. Of course I didn't know at the time that Navy Pier would play an important role in my professional career! My classmates included returning war veterans taking advantage of the GI bill, so it was an older and more serious group of students. After studying, we would enjoy the bars and restaurants nearby, and we developed friendships that continue to this day.

After graduating from U. of I. in 1952 and passing the state board examination, I joined the architectural firm of Naess and Murphy. During this period, I had the opportunity to work on the plans for the Prudential Building. This was Chicago's first post-war high-rise and also the first one built directly over the IC tracks.

In 1960, I began a lengthy career of public service with the city of Chicago. I was appointed City Architect under Mayors Richard J. Daley and Michael Bilandic, Commissioner of Public Works under Jane Byrne, and Commissioner of Aviation under Harold Washington.

Under Richard J. Daley, we initiated a number of plans aimed at preserving and strengthening Chicago's central area. Our downtown area was becoming an office center, and residents were fleeing to the suburbs. At nights and on weekends, downtown was dead. Like other cities, Chicago was looking for the magic formula to bring people back.

In 1973, Mayor Daley endorsed a plan called "Chicago 21." Among other things, this ambitious plan included developing the underutilized railway yards around the downtown area for new projects. Dearborn Park, a "new town within the city" on abandoned rail yards south of the Loop, was a dramatic success. And then there were projects involving the adaptive reuse of older buildings. One of these was Dearborn Green—the rehab of old loft buildings for housing and mixed use in Printer's Row. People living on the perimeter of the Loop would now be able to walk to work.

Another expansion of Chicago's central area, this one east of Michigan Avenue, was a challenge because we didn't want to risk despoiling the lakefront. The Illinois Center Air Rights development was built over 84 acres of railway yards between the Loop and Lake Michigan. We designed a massive new multilevel roadway project that included extending Wacker Drive east of Michigan Avenue, and Columbus Drive north from Monroe Street across the Chicago River on a new bascule bridge. We also eliminated the treacherous Lake Shore Drive "S" curve.

When we started to think about redeveloping Navy Pier, not much had been built east of Michigan Avenue. The Pier opened in 1916 as a terminal for Great Lakes shipping and a public recreation facility. Over the years it hosted Pageants of Progress, a navy training facility, international trade shows, the Chicago campus of U. of I., and numerous municipal gatherings and public events. When the first McCormick Place was destroyed by fire in 1967, Navy Pier saved the day by housing trade shows and exhibitions until the new McCormick Place opened in 1971.

Richard J. Daley always felt that the Pier was important to the city. He really wanted to see something happen and decided to have the city restore the Pier's east end buildings as a bicentennial project. That project won a national award for design excellence from the American Institute of Architects, and City Council designated Navy Pier an official Chicago

The completed State Street Mall was dedicated on October 29, 1979. Commissioner of Public Works Jerome R. Butler (left) shared the podium with Mayor Jane M. Byrne and Arthur E. Osborne (Chicago Public Library, Special Collections and Preservation Division).

Eric Bronsky built this scale model of the Illinois Central Air Rights development for the Department of Public Works in 1980. It depicts the realigned Lake Shore Drive S-curve (right) and a new network of multilevel roadways. Michigan Avenue is just beyond the left side of the photo, and Monroe Street is in the bottom foreground. The IC Suburban tracks at lower left was the future site of Millennium Park (Eric Bronsky photo).

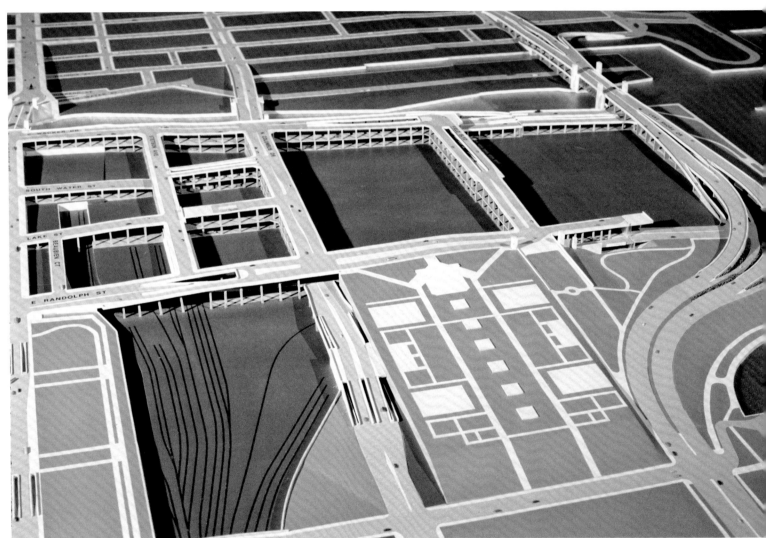

"There is a cohesiveness about this city that I don't think you find in any other major city."
Potter Palmer IV

landmark. In 1979, it was also listed in the National Register of Historic Places.

During the summers of 1978 through 1981, Mayor Jane Byrne held ChicagoFests at Navy Pier. Studies and proposals to further redevelop the Pier were sidelined for the remainder of the eighties while City Hall was preoccupied with "Council Wars." It wasn't until 1990, after creation of the MPEA (Metropolitan Pier and Exposition Authority), that the city and state joined forces to resume redevelopment plans. After I left city government, the MPEA retained me as a consultant and later I joined them as the first general manager of the new Navy Pier. I served in that capacity during the reconstruction period and its initial years of operation.

Today, Navy Pier attracts over nine million visitors annually and is the number one tourist attraction in Illinois. I think it's been a major factor in getting people reacquainted with the central area of Chicago. However, not all aspects of the Pier have been as successful as we originally envisioned. The need for new sources of revenue should be balanced with public uses—keep in mind that the principal attraction of the Pier is the lakefront itself.

It's interesting to see how the Navy Pier redevelopment is used as a marketing tool for all the new condominium residences that are being built in the central area. Open the Sunday Chicago Tribune real estate section and chances are you'll see a view from a condo looking towards Navy Pier.

Another problem that we began to address during the Richard J. Daley administration was State Street. Chicago wasn't alone during this period of urban decline—cities around the country were looking for strategies to attract tourists and residents back to the city. There was a national trend to close off main streets to cars and provide buses or light rail transit; these were called transit malls. The idea for State Street was to provide an attractive environment for pedestrians where they didn't have to fight auto traffic to get to the stores.

The downtown businesses and the State Street Council urged the city to obtain federal funding. They began the project in mid-1978 and completed it in October 1979. The roadway was narrowed to two bus lanes with a third lane for boarding at intersections. The mall included new sidewalks, street surfaces, lighting, and landscaping. Subway entrances were remodeled with enclosures, and shelters were built at bus waiting areas.

The new mall improved pedestrian circulation and bus flow, reduced air pollution, and resulted in an improved appearance. However, it failed to stimulate the street's economy and thus was perceived to be a failure. So, the State Street Council and city once again renovated State Street, reopening it to auto traffic in November 1996.

With more people now living downtown, I believe State Street will continue to change for the better. Although the street still has problems as illustrated by recent department store closings, there are some positive signs. For example, the exterior of Carson's was recently restored and now, rather than serving solely as a department store, the interior is undergoing an adaptive reuse as an office and retail complex. There is even some residential use of the street, with student housing on the upper floors of some of the historic buildings.

Possibly the most important new development on State Street, though, is the long anticipated redevelopment of Block 37. This project includes an office tower, a retail mall, two residential towers, and a transportation center that includes a new subway station which will provide a central departure point for passengers bound for either O'Hare or Midway Airports. This project promises to breathe new life into State Street as well as the central business district. So, the mall was just one brief snapshot in time during the street's ongoing evolution.

The extension of Wacker Drive east of Michigan Avenue was completed in three stages. In 1969, the steelwork was begun to extend Wacker just 300 feet to provide access to the new 111 E. Wacker building. As published in the *Chicago Sun-Times*. Photographer unknown (Copyright 1969 by Chicago Sun-Times, Inc. Reprinted with permission).

In the early '70s, the city was planning a "Central Area Transit System" that included adding new subway routes to the Near North Side and McCormick Place, and eventually eliminating the entire Loop "L" structure. Fortunately, or unfortunately, depending on your point of view, this project never became a reality. Later on, I was involved with a proposal for the "Central Area Circulator," a light-rail transit network. I really think the city should have stuck with architect Harry Weese's original idea for a riverfront transit line. His plan was for the route to start in Pilsen and run along the river on an existing railroad right-of-way, connecting the commuter railroad stations with the Merchandise Mart, State Street, Michigan Avenue, and Navy Pier. The beauty of his plan was its low cost, with relatively little land acquisition needed. One obvious benefit would have been reducing the number of cars that park on the lakefront.

But no, the plan evolved into something different, larger, and much more expensive. Frankly I was concerned about light rail transit operating on streets throughout the Loop. In the end, federal funding for mass transit lines was drying up and the project failed to obtain funds.

As for the city's lakefront, Chicago is blessed with two great natural assets—the lake and the river. Very few cities in North America have a lakefront like Chicago—Toronto is the only one that comes to mind. Cleveland didn't protect their lakefront; it's industrial, and as a result nobody lives downtown and the office buildings are half-empty.

Initially, Chicago didn't protect its lakefront either—in 1852 they let the Illinois Central Railroad run its tracks into downtown right along the shore. You look at early photos, and everything from Michigan Avenue east is just solid railroad tracks all the way out to Navy Pier. It was certainly an unwise decision, but one that Chicago learned from.

Over the years, planners and architects sought to cover those unattractive railroad tracks at Chicago's front door. I remember standing on the balcony of the Cliff Dwellers Club on Michigan Avenue with my friend Ira Bach, who was commissioner of the Planning Department, discussing this very thing. In the mid 1990s, the city negotiated an agreement with the Illinois Central Railroad to return the unused lakefront land north of McCormick Place to the city. This cleared the way to transform the unsightly railroad tracks and parking lots that had blighted this prime area for so many years.

In 2004, Millennium Park was completed. It was unique, being built on a structural platform over commuter railroad tracks and a parking garage. On top is a new type of urban park that's an interesting contrast to the Beaux Arts style of Grant Park. It's an amazing engineering accomplishment and a wonderful addition to the lakefront and Chicago's downtown.

Grant Park is without question one of Chicago's principal downtown parks, thanks to Montgomery Ward, a prominent Chicagoan who led the fight for the park to remain forever open. Today, Grant Park has become all the more important because of the high-rise development that has occurred at both ends of the park, framing it like a pair of bookends. With the boom in condo towers and people living downtown, this open space is becoming more vital to the continued success of our central area.

Other planning efforts since the 1960s led to the creation of several plazas or open spaces in the central area, including Civic (Daley) Center Plaza and Federal Center Plaza. Although some of these plazas have fountains and sculptures by world renowned artists, there are actually few amenities for pedestrians. The city should take its cue from the success of Millennium Park and consider adding trees, benches, and sidewalk cafes to these places.

following pages
Michigan Avenue, looking south towards the completed first stage of the Wacker Drive extension in 1972. Michigan had recently been improved. As published in the *Chicago Sun-Times*. Photographer: Gene Pesek (Copyright 1972 by Chicago Sun-Times, Inc. Reprinted with permission).

The second extension, which linked Wacker Drive with Stetson and the old Lake Shore Drive S-Curve, was completed in 1975. The final stage was completed in 1986, in tandem with the realignment of the S-curve. As published in the *Chicago Sun-Times*. Photographer: Bob Fila (Copyright 1975 by Chicago Sun-Times, Inc. Reprinted with permission).

Looking at the overall picture, I think several factors worked together to insure the survival and rebirth of Chicago's downtown. Chicago was once a wild and wooly place. The transition from a slaughterhouse to a city of elegant neighborhoods was a gradual one. The 'City Beautiful' movement, which came from the Century of Progress, had a big impact, and of course, Daniel Burnham's Plan of 1909 also paved the way.

Chicago school students once studied a textbook called *Wacker's Manual,* which was an abridged version of the Plan of 1909. So, the kids who would become tomorrow's civic leaders learned at an early age what this Plan was all about. The funny part is, when Burnham prepared his *Plan of Chicago,* nobody was building high-rises, so there were no high-rises in his Plan! Other things, too, never happened in quite the way they were envisioned in the Plan. For example, City Hall would have been at Halsted and Congress.

Much more recently, events like ChicagoFest and projects like the redevelopment of Navy Pier got people to understand the benefits of living downtown, where they would be close to its cultural institutions and other attractions. That's what finally tipped the scales and convinced developers and investors to build those condo towers. The empty nesters were coming back to the city, and universities were converting old commercial buildings into student housing.

As for what is needed to insure the continued success of Chicago's central area, that's difficult to answer. Certainly, many issues are important to the future of our city. Because of my background as an architect and Public Works administrator, I'm inclined to stress the need for good public transportation and well-maintained infrastructure as critical.

Transit problems have contributed to the deterioration of our nation's cities in the past. Today, much of Chicago's transit system is old and appears to be in need of maintenance, improvements, and expansion. How well we solve our transportation problems is one of the key issues that could impact how downtown Chicago will fare in the future.

You have to continually invest in your infrastructure because everything gets old. But, Chicago is making progress on cleaning up and beautifying downtown streets, the river, and of course, the lakefront. It's great to see how many developers are now looking at sites that they might have ignored in the past, but we also have to preserve and protect public open space along the lakefront and the river from being completely swallowed up by private use.

I doubt whether we'll ever end the love affair with cars in America. But when you consider our nation's energy problems, environmental problems in our urban centers, and the automobile's contribution to air pollution, it seems obvious to me that we should give the highest priority to maintaining and improving our mass transit systems.

Marshall Field V

I visited Chicago a couple of times when I was just a young kid, but the only memory I have of downtown was being taken to Marshall Field and Company for Christmas to eat lunch in the Walnut Room. That was really the only thing I did in Chicago, although my father also may have taken me to Lincoln Park Zoo a couple of times. But, I spent more time in the *Sun-Times* office just running around the offices when I was little. I have no real memories of downtown or State Street except that there were grey, amorphous, old dark buildings with no appeal to me whatsoever.

I wasn't going to volunteer to go downtown, and except for visiting Field's, I just never went. As for Field's at Christmastime, I remember the windows being great and, to me, there were two great department stores: Field's and Macy's. I knew about Macy's because I had grown up on the East Coast.

My parents were divorced when I was young, so I didn't move to Chicago until I was 24 years old, in 1965, and that makes me a relative newcomer to the city. My father died when he was just 49 years old, so I moved to Chicago to become the publisher of the *Chicago Sun-Times*. In preparation for that role, I decided to spend a year and a half to two years working for a while in all of the different divisions of the newspaper so I would at least have some idea of what was going on. Then, I took over the paper. I was there for 15 years, and when I resigned, I selected Jim Hoge to fill that role. That lasted a year until my brother came along and said that I had to sell the company. My brother and I had made an agreement on the split-up that whoever offered us the highest price for the newspaper we would sell it to that person or company. So, both of our hands were tied. Rupert Murdoch offered us the most money, so he became the new owner of the paper and decided not to retain Hoge. I now look out the windows of my current office on Wacker Drive, and I can see the paper located across the river. It tells me that it was a good business decision to get out of owning the paper ten years ago.

When I came to Chicago to run the *Sun-Times,* I didn't really think that downtown, which to me was south of the river, had particularly changed much. Really, most of the change came in the last years of Mayor Richard J. Daley's mayoralty, and then continued through the Byrne, Sawyer, and Washington periods in office. For whatever reason, Chicago caught on, I think partly because a lot of the big law firms pushed for the demolition of aging buildings and the construction of new ones. There were buildings that stuck out in everybody's mind like the Standard Oil Building, the John Hancock Building (which is in the wrong location), a couple of the newer downtown buildings, and, finally, the Sears Tower. After the big growth period, construction downtown seemed to stop for a while because people had new buildings, and those who constructed new buildings were unhappy about the financial situation. The worst part of that period happened in the late '80s and early '90s. We were in the real estate business in other towns, and we got "killed" financially, just like everyone else. And, similar to other cities, Chicago became overbuilt. Now that has happened with apartment buildings, and you will see some of those buildings go back to the banks. As for the condo boom, once the developers and builders get their bank money and start construction, you can't stop or you hand the buildings back to the bank.

I thought that the State Street Mall was kind of a joke because there wasn't anything down there except for sort of "has-beens." In my judgment, the thing that started the turnaround in the '90s were things like the School of the Art Institute and Roosevelt University, which picked that moment to buy and rehab or build new buildings and dormitories downtown. I think that brought young people downtown and the students were living there. Nobody lived in those buildings until then, and you couldn't make a community. And now might be a good time for the so-called Mall, but it's just too late.

I think that the crowning achievement of the new downtown was the building of Millennium Park, which has changed South Michigan Avenue from nothing to becoming a desirable place to be. A lot of the newly developed downtown areas are populated by old people from the suburbs and new people like the students and a younger generation. I think that is due

CHICAGO
$2 TO 11AM DAILY
TERROR STALKS IN
HE KNOWS
YOU'RE ALONE
& INVASION OF
THE BODY
SNATCHERS
STATE LA

to Mayor Richard M. Daley, who loves the city. The result has become that Chicago is not only a city that works but a great city to live in because it has been beautified. I just think that's great.

I was running the newspaper during many of the days when Richard J. Daley was mayor of Chicago. He would visit the paper about twice a year for a general discussion, and it always ended up with him angry at the *Sun-Times* because we were constantly printing exposés that led to his friends being put in jail. He wasn't averse to giving people hell, and we would say to him, "Mr. Mayor, if your friend wasn't a crook, he wouldn't have gone to jail." He responded, "Well, I just don't know that." I think that Richie actually is a better mayor than his father. But it's all a matter of timing. The beginning of the change in the downtown was during Richard J. Daley's terms of office. I would argue that Chicago is one of the great cities in the world simply because you can do a lot of business here. However, Chicago has changed. It is no longer a major transportation hub, but it is really a place with good service businesses. Unfortunately, many of the major companies are located on the ring around the city, and the lawyers commute into and out of the city.

The only worry I have is that as you push the computer age, more and more people are going to work out of their homes. In this day and age, I wouldn't build a new building to own because I am really worried that, over the next 40 years, some of my children and grandchildren are going to stay home in droves because it's going to save the company money to have you work at home and not need an office. I just think that is an important trend in the development of new buildings for downtown. It means that companies will have less need for business and office buildings. On the other hand, thanks to the museums and some of the stores having a comeback, downtown will continue to grow as a residential place and you may see some of the "B" office buildings rehabbed and turned into apartments.

I also don't know how much more Chicago tourism can continue to grow. I think that the world at large knows not to go to Chicago in winter. So, we only have April through October as a viable tourist season. And just driving around, we are already stuffed with people in the downtown area, and I don't think that downtown is a big attraction for tourists. Rather, they are interested in the museums, Navy Pier, and Millennium Park. As far as downtown is concerned, I don't think that it is going to be affected one way or the other. However, there will be more housing located there.

I don't have the sense that State Street is changing one way or the other. My biggest worry is that I don't see the amenities available for people who have moved downtown. There was supposed to be a big shopping center for people living there, but it hasn't been built. So, where do you go for your grocery shopping if you live downtown? I think that has to be addressed. However, there are a few good restaurants downtown like the Italian Village, Berghoff's, and Petterino's, and others that are popular and meet the needs of residents. I think that people who live in the Loop don't want to travel too far north or south.

Chicago's downtown has survived, unlike other big city downtowns such as Detroit, Cleveland, and Los Angeles, due to a mayor who really cares about the city and who has been great. I was up in Detroit recently, and I think that some of these things are beyond saving because their critical industry has basically moved away from that city. So, all you have is what's left, and they are doing badly There are no "drivers" in Detroit. The driving force in Chicago has been the huge development of the suburbs that forced service companies to locate somewhere. Those service companies decided that being located in the city would leave them equidistant from places like Naperville and Des Plaines. I think that one or two companies like Boeing stayed, and that was a huge deal. They picked Chicago's downtown because it is a higher status area than being in Elgin or near O'Hare Airport.

I don't see the Loop getting weaker because as soon as real estate gets in trouble and people start dropping the rents, eventually, it comes closer to being equal to the fancy rents in the suburbs. Somebody will realize that they can move for nothing, but will decide to move downtown where there are amenities for their workforce. Also, the traffic is just as bad in the suburbs as it is downtown. I think that we are going to be okay.

I don't think that Chicago is a "tough" city...climate aside. It really is an easy city, and people here are warm, open, and responsive neighbors unlike Boston and New York. I can just tell you that when I moved to Chicago, people for whom I could do nothing went out of their way to make me feel welcome. The reason that the city works so well is that both Mayor Richard J. Daley and Mayor Richard M. Daley have encouraged the business leaders of Chicago to participate in the life of the city. So, if the mayor wants to get something done, he gets hold of three or four people, and they can organize around such projects as bringing the Olympics to Chicago. There is an atmosphere here in which everyone who is in a leadership role participates in something. That is not necessarily true in other places like New York or Boston. I think that Chicago is outstanding as a city.

Potter Palmer IV

During the 1960s, I had an office downtown in my family offices at the old Railway Exchange Building and was living in Lake Forest by then with my wife, son, and daughter. I was managing family affairs, even though I was starting to do get involved in other business activities of my own. When the '68 Democratic National Convention took place, I was floored by what was happening and I wasn't the only one to have that reaction. I remember watching it on television and being aghast by what some people were doing to the city and how they were behaving. I think we all grew up a lot during that week.

As for the State Street Mall, I remember that before it was built I had mental images of a major street being converted into a beautiful, park-like mall. And when it was finished, I remember looking at the "mall" and thinking "Is this all there is?" Certainly, it was a nicer street and it wasn't so busy with traffic, but it looked substantially the same to me. I felt that all the fuss over such a minor change perhaps hadn't been worth the effort. It had little impact on State Street and certainly didn't meet my expectations. I thought that there wasn't going to be any automotive traffic, even the buses, but I turned out to be wrong. I felt that the project was more hype than anything else.

I don't know if there is a special responsibility with having the name and legacy of being Potter Palmer, but I am involved in Chicago's civic affairs and have been on the board of a number of organizations. I am currently on the board of the Chicago History Museum and a small not-for-profit named Artistic Circles, and was formerly on the board of the Art Institute. I don't remember going there a lot when I was growing up, even though my family donated a lot of works of art to it and my grandfather was president of the board of directors.

In respect to the issue of the future of downtown, I don't think that the Loop will become a blight on the city. There is still the Palmer House as well as other hotels, major banks and financial institutions, and Macy's. I still think of it as Marshall Field's. If you compare downtown Chicago with other major American cities where many have fled the city's center, like Detroit, I don't see it happening in our city. However, as far as retail shopping, some of the old department stores have opened branches, or, in some cases, have moved off of State Street and entirely out of the Loop. But, it is still busy down there during the daytime and there is legitimate theatre available in the evening.

I remember when some friends of mine came to visit us during the early '60s from New York City and wanted to go into the city from Lake Forest. I scratched my head and thought, "Where are we going to go?" The only place I could think of was the Palmer House since the only decent places to eat were hotel dining rooms. That has all changed, and younger people are now staying in Chicago or moving to the city because it has so much to offer.

I think that we are lucky to live in a vibrant city with a downtown that is active. Mayor Richard M. Daley and some of his predecessors have worked very closely with all of the elements of the city of Chicago, including the civic, religious, and business leaders. There is cohesiveness about this city that I don't think you find in any other major city because, in Chicago, everybody knows each other and can work closely with people from the various elements of society. To the extent that whoever is mayor can pick up the phone and call any of those individuals or groups, I think that downtown and the city are going to be fine. However, if that ever starts to fragment, then I don't know what will happen.

The new State of Illinois building under construction at LaSalle and Lake in early 1982. Within the next five years, the old buildings behind the "L" would also be replaced (Eric Bronsky photo).

The focal point of the outdoor plaza at One Financial Place, built on the site of LaSalle Street Station, is the sculpture, *San Marco II*, by Ludovico di Luigi. Philip Johnson's trendsetting 190 South LaSalle building is in the background (Eric Bronsky photo).

In this 1997 view of Plymouth Court looking south from Jackson, the postmodern Harold Washington Library looms over Binyon's Restaurant, which had recently closed (Eric Bronsky photo).

James McDonough

My view of the State Street Mall is that in its original stage, it was not a bad idea. That idea came into play under Jane Byrne, but it started under Richard J. Daley. The problem with having an open mall where people could walk up and down State Street was that it really disrupted the flow of traffic. Also, most of the stores started closing or deteriorating, except for Carson's and Field's. Some of the structures became almost "honky-tonk" in nature, and that was the major downfall of the Mall.

Then, of course, the city decided to give up the idea and go back to cars on the street. I don't know what difference it has made since State Street is still going downhill as a shopping area. I think that South Michigan Avenue will have a comeback, both in terms of retail and housing.

I remember the big flood of the Chicago River into portions of downtown, and that was the strangest thing. There was a contractor who breached an abandoned freight tunnel under the river that ended up flooding downtown. A couple of the divers working to fill the hole were almost drowned down there, and we were there day and night. In response to the flood, Mayor Richard M. Daley fired the commissioner of Public Works because he wasn't there to manage everything. It was a scary situation. Downtown was very much in danger because of the flood, and we were very concerned that if it went on much longer it could have taken some buildings out.

Chicago's downtown is unique as compared with other major cities because it is a very clean city...amazingly clean. Of course I was commissioner of Streets and Sanitation, so I have a certain bias on the topic, but when you go to New York and there are bags of garbage on the street because they don't have alleys, you really appreciate Chicago for being so clean. What a lot of people didn't know about downtown is that we used to send out crews early in the morning. The crews included mechanical sweepers as well as hand sweepers. Daley was almost fanatical about keeping downtown clean. Downtown was also well-policed, and it was kept as a pleasant place to be and for visitors, and generally you felt safe when you were there.

Both of the Daley mayors were tough administrators who loved the job and lived it 24 hours a day. It was clear to me that if you didn't share this feeling, you would have a short career. When Jane Byrne was elected mayor over Mike Bilandic, I was chairman of the CTA and a target because of my past association with the Daley family. At her request, I resigned as chairman but remained as a board member until the end of my term.

Many medium and big city downtowns "died" during the '50s and '60s, and Chicago's downtown also struggled and deteriorated but still kept going despite the closing of several major department stores. I think that Chicago's downtown survived because it was still a pleasant and clean place, and they continued to have various functions and parades that were still held around downtown. And Richard J. Daley, being a very persuasive person, helped to keep downtown alive. If he wanted something, he could make things happen with the business community, and he could get some of the city's "heavyweights" to support his ideas.

As for downtown's present day problems, crime is always a major concern. The problem now on State Street is one of the "quality" of the stores that remain in business. There are some junky places along State Street and even Michigan Avenue. I suppose that the move downtown of people from the suburbs who are buying residences there is a good thing. However, I don't know how long people are going to stay. You've got 22-year old kids buying $400,000 condominiums, and I think that somewhere along the line they are going to have a problem selling those places. Also, parking is a major, major concern when people come downtown today.

The Pacific Garden Mission, located on State Street near Harrison, is one of the last remnants of the South Loop's historical propensity to the poor and homeless (Eric Bronsky photo).

Blighted areas on the outer fringes of the Loop are rapidly disappearing, but along this stretch of Clark Street between Van Buren and Congress change has been slow to arrive. Perhaps its close proximity to the Metropolitan Correctional Center (not visible in this view) is why (Eric Bronsky photo).

Richard J. Daley delivers a victory speech following his reelection to a sixth term as mayor of Chicago on April 2, 1975. Left to right: Daley's daughter, Mrs. Patricia Thompson; son William; daughter-in-law Margaret "Maggie" Daley and her husband Richard M. (behind Eleanor "Sis" Daley); and son John. Originally published in the *Chicago Daily News*. Photographer: Edmund Jarecki (Copyright 1975 by Chicago Sun-Times, Inc. Reprinted with permission).

Mayor Richard M. Daley, flanked by (left to right) State Representative Monique Davis, Denise Casalino, Illinois Governor George Ryan and State Representative Mary Flowers, cuts the ribbon at a ceremony on a frigid November 26, 2002 for the reopening of Wacker Drive following its reconstruction. As published in the *Chicago Sun-Times*. Photographer: Brian Jackson (Copyright 2002 by Chicago Sun-Times, Inc. Reprinted with permission).

Myles Jarrow

Today, I go downtown as little as possible, primarily because of congestion and the high cost of parking. When I tell people outside of Chicago what the typical parking rates are, they're absolutely astounded. Recently I went downtown for a doctor appointment. I was in his office for only 70-75 minutes, but it cost $23 to park my car! Those rates are ridiculous!

I will say one thing about Chicago: The fourteen commuter rail lines radiating out from downtown certainly keep a lot of traffic off the road. Before they were all coordinated under the RTA, if any one of the commuter railroads was on strike and service was not operating, you could certainly notice the increase in traffic leading in that direction. Between the commuter railroads and CTA, Chicago is extremely fortunate to have what I feel is a good public transportation system.

A number of things kept Chicago alive while other cities were dying. First, we have many diverse types of industries here—we're not dependent upon one industry alone. I think Detroit's dependency on the automobile industry was the factor that led to the downfall of that city's central business district.

And, once again, we do have very good transportation facilities. Our geographical position at the tip of Lake Michigan, which extends so far south into the U.S., makes it necessary to travel through Chicago, and that's why Chicago became the nation's transportation hub. As a result, the railroads have been a major industry for Chicago over the years. As long as commerce is transported by the railroads, Chicago should remain in very good shape.

Then, large companies, such as Boeing, have chosen to settle in Chicago. There seems to be a constant flow—some companies leave but others come in, so it appears that Chicago will remain vital and viable.

Finally, Chicago is blessed with a number of very fine world-class museums, which brings a lot of visitors to Chicago. We certainly have plenty of hotel accommodations for them, sometimes at extremely high prices, but they're available. What the current Mayor Daley has done to beautify the streets of Chicago is highly commendable. Projects like North LaSalle Street with its center parkway and planters certainly improve the surroundings.

top

Though it's role as the nation's rail hub has diminished, Chicago continues to maintain a comprehensive network of commuter and intercity passenger railroad routes that radiate out from downtown in all directions. Emerging from beneath the Post Office in this 1977 view are a Burlington Northern (now Metra) commuter train and an Amtrak intercity train (George E. Kanary photo).

center left

South of Millennium Park, tracks are still visible along the lakefront. An outbound South Shore Line train (left) stops to board passengers at Van Buren while a string of Metra Electric "Highliners" rests on a storage track (Eric Bronsky photo).

center right

The newly rebuilt entrance to the Grant Park Underground Garage on Michigan Boulevard, looking south from Washington. The kiosk on the sidewalk is the pedestrian entrance to the garage (Eric Bronsky photo).

bottom

Sleek condominium and office towers rise behind the magnificently restored Chicago Cultural Center at Michigan and Washington (Eric Bronsky photo).

James O'Connor

Our downtown is different from other cities because of the concentration of activity in a relatively small area. That makes it somewhat unique, and is particularly true today with the return of the legitimate theatres like the Ford, LaSalle, and Goodman Theatres. They have all made the nighttime activities much better than they had been in the past. We did go through a down period before these positive changes and now people are more comfortable about staying after hours. The additions of Millennium Park, Navy Pier, and Northerly Island have all made a huge difference.

I think that a lot of these positive changes can be traced to the political leadership of the city and both Mayor Daleys. Chicago has always been clean, and that is a real plus. I've been in some cities that I did not feel were anywhere near as clean as Chicago. I also think that security downtown has generally always been good. Of course, as I grew up, I was downtown a lot and I was never concerned about my personal safety. I'm not sure that was a common view of things in the '60s and '70s. The perception of safety today is important, and people seem to have confidence in Chicago's law enforcement. People also think that Chicago is a "green" city, which it was not before all the plantings done by Mayor Daley in recent years. They had added a great deal to the city and made it a much more attractive place to be.

In part, Chicago got cleaner as there was the shift away from coal burning. Back in the '60s and '70s, we had a lot of coal-fired facilities run by Commonwealth Edison. We started by putting precipitators on the smokestacks that took the dust out of the air. Then, Commonwealth Edison began to burn low sulfur coal that we got from Wyoming and Montana and brought to the city in 100-car trains everyday. Also, there is now a renewed call for nuclear power.

Chicago does have a reputation for "toughness" and getting things done. I think that we have a very proactive mayor who is also into the details of things, and for him, it is not just a vision but a day-to-day style where he constantly takes care of the little issues. He gives the citizens the belief that the city is on the way up. It is amazing that when I talk to friends from across the country who haven't been to Chicago in 10-20 years but are coming back to visit. They are just amazed at how good the city feels. There are now places like the Peninsula Hotel, a world-class, signature hotel on the near North Side, as well as the Four Seasons and the Ritz-Carlton Hotels, which are considered among the best hotels in the world. Chicago now has a great complement for housing people, as well as a pretty good transportation system. I think that people like being in Chicago.

Downtown's present day problems include the need to continue to find new things that will cause people to want to come into the Loop and its environs. Now, just trying to drive into the city from the suburbs on the weekends has become almost impossible. So, something must be happening because people are not only going to sports events. They are coming to the restaurants, the theatres, and just coming downtown to stroll in places like Millennium Park. Those places weren't here until recent years. I think that is a real plus for us. As for people moving downtown, we were one of those couples who have made the move back to the city from the suburbs. We are very happy that we made the move, and we are out almost every night at places like the Shakespeare Theatre, the Steppenwolf, or the opera and symphony. I do think that those sorts of attractions have made the difference, and there is just a lot of stuff happening downtown.

I believe that in the next 25 years, the future of downtown will be stronger than ever. When you look at the new housing that is going up on the Near South Side, from Roosevelt Road southward, that was a wasteland and where the slums were located. It all started with Dearborn Park, although a lot of people never thought it would get off the ground. Now it is not just a bunch of apartment complexes. There is a school located there and an infrastructure that includes good restaurants and shopping. The same thing is happening on the West Side and the Northwest Side. And, homes around Division and the Kennedy Expressway that were selling for $60,000 some 15 years ago are now selling from $600,000 to $1 million today in the same neighborhoods. The opportunity to buy those properties is probably driven by the ever-growing phenomenon of "two-income" families, as well as the amenities that are available to those who live downtown.

When State Street was rebuilt in the mid-90s to restore auto traffic,
beautification of pedestrian spaces received top consideration.
The once-grim stretch from Van Buren to Congress is now dominated by
the Harold Washington Library (left) and Robert Morris College in the
former Sears building at right (Eric Bronsky photo).

State Street, looking north towards Quincy, still tends to be quiet on
weekends but nonetheless appears attractive and inviting (Eric Bronsky photo).

Optimistic about the future of State Street, Sears moved back downtown,
opening a brand new flagship store at the northwest corner of State
and Madison in 2000. This same building once housed the Boston Store and
later Walgreen's (Eric Bronsky photo).

Randolph Street looking west from State in 1933 (courtesy of the Chicago Transit Authority)

Randolph Street looking west from State in 2007. Everything except Marshall Field's clock and the Oriental Theatre sign is different, and new construction is finally rising on long-vacant Block 37 (Eric Bronsky photo).

"I think that the crowning achievement of the new downtown was the building of Millennium Park, which has changed South Michigan Avenue from nothing to becoming a desirable place to be."
Marshall Field V

Ornate shelters over the subway entrances, combined with occasional touches of whimsy and other "retro" elements such as an old-fashioned style of street lights, blend in well with the historic flavor of State Street's architectural treasures (Eric Bronsky photo).

During Jane Byrne's term as mayor, the City's official Christmas tree was briefly relocated from Daley Center to the intersection of State and Wacker (Eric Bronsky photo).

Sculpture, *Cloud Gate* by Anish Kapoor, in Millennium Park (Eric Bronsky photo).

The serpentine BP Bridge over Columbus Drive that leads into Millennium Park and the Jay Pritzker Pavilion in the background were designed by architect Frank Gehry (Eric Bronsky photo).

"Chicago's front door" aptly describes the city's lakefront whose skyline view is unmatched anywhere else (Eric Bronsky photo).

Buckingham Fountain (photo by Eric Bronsky photo).

A puzzled seagull scrutinizes a Segway tour pausing at Buckingham Fountain (Eric Bronsky photo).

next page
Downtown's skyline, looking north along Clark Street from 18th in the South Loop area (Eric Bronsky photo).

Downtown's skyline viewed from Paulina and the Eisenhower Expressway on the Near West Side (Eric Bronsky photo).

Perhaps no other photo of present-day Chicago sums up the reconnecting of the city with its spectacular lakefront than this aerial view of Navy Pier (City of Chicago photo by Peter Schulz, courtesy of Jerome R. Butler).

"The waterfront is where most of our country's older cities originally started, and once again it's the waterfronts where some of the most significant new redevelopment has occurred. But few cities have protected their waterfront as well as Chicago. We are very fortunate that our lakefront and the Chicago River continue to be among the city's most valuable resources." *Jerome R. Butler*

PART V
EPILOGUE

And Then There Were Two

Chicago's pride, muscular resolve, and ability to bounce back from hard times are legendary. But downtown continues to flow with the proverbial river current of evolution. Every day, month, week, or year is but a brief snapshot in time, and over the span of several decades, little has remained untouched. Today's downtown is a much different place than 100, 50, or even 25 years ago.

Not every change has been positive. Chicago's bold reputation for getting things done all too often translates into moving brashly ahead at the expense of tradition. Banal fortress-like towers have replaced many of the architectural treasures, and carbon-copy national entities have been edging out charismatic local icons.

To all but the most astute observer, today's downtown appears cosmopolitan, prosperous, clean, and actually quite inviting. But to some longtime Chicago residents, even taking into consideration marvelous new attractions like Millennium Park, downtown no longer feels like the special place it once was. Perhaps it is because the few remaining elements that link Chicago's downtown with its past or otherwise convey a sense of local uniqueness or identity are gradually disappearing. Sadly, this trend is not diminishing. Within a relatively brief time span, three revered institutions that were part of downtown Chicago's fabric for over a century unexpectedly and abruptly changed course or disappeared altogether.

Without question, the most poignant loss was Marshall Field's. A traditional family-owned department store chain made legendary by its retailing innovations, quality goods, and superlative customer service for over 150 years, Field's had passed through a succession of ownerships since 1982. Despite changes for better or for worse, the palatial State Street store, a landmark that had become synonymous with Chicago, ranked with Navy Pier and the Museum of Science and Industry as one of the city's top attractions for both local residents and tourists.

In 2005 Macy's Group Inc.* purchased Marshall Field's. Known for acquiring regional department store chains and converting them to the national Macy's brand, the company at first believed that converting these stores would not alienate Chicagoans. Moreover, they planned to retain the Walnut Room, Frango Mints, and other Field's traditions. When the conversion was completed on September 9, 2006, Marshall Field's passed into history.

In the past, shuttering a Loop department store would elicit little more than a whimper. But the public reaction to this change was stronger than anticipated. Initially confident that their marketing strategy would soon win over former Field's shoppers, Macy's eventually realized that their formula, which had been successful elsewhere, was not working in Chicago. By mid-2007 there were rumors that more changes were in the works for the State Street landmark.

Meanwhile, in December 2005, the third-generation owners of the 107-year-old Berghoff Restaurant announced their intention to retire and close the legendary German eatery at the end of February 2006. The building was to remain in the family because their daughter leased the space for her own company, Artistic Events by Carlyn Berghoff Catering, Inc. Over the next two months, thousands of mournful customers waited in long lines that at times stretched around the corner onto Dearborn Street for the opportunity to indulge in one final platter of hearty German fare. A few days after the restaurant closed, nostalgic customers bid princely sums at an auction of the restaurant's memorabilia.

*Macy's Group Inc. was known as Federated Department Stores Inc. prior to June 2007.

previous page
Field's south atrium and the celebrated Tiffany dome.

Main entrance to Marshall Field's on State Street

Store directory and Field family coat of arms on an elevator door

Shoppers gaze upward to admire the Tiffany dome

Marshall Field's Walnut Room in February 2006

The Berghoff Restaurant in January 2006.

Longtime maitre d' Mike Santiago strikes a familiar pose
at the entrance to the Old Heidelberg Room.

One of many waiters who had worked at the Berghoff for
decades. As published in the *Chicago Sun-Times*. Photographer:
Al Podgorski (Copyright 2006 by Chicago Sun-Times, Inc.
Reprinted with permission).

Renamed the Century Room, the former restaurant's main dining
room now serves as a stately venue for private parties but
still opens to the public for traditional Christmas dining and events.
(courtesy of Artistic Events by Carlyn Berghoff Catering, Inc.).

The sense of loss was short-lived as that stretch of Adams Street didn't remain quiet for very long. The fourth-generation owner promptly went to work, opening the Berghoff Café on the lower level in April, and then 17/west at the Berghoff on the main floor. Today, not only can you once again tip back a stein of Berghoff's famous draft beer and enjoy a hand-carved sandwich in the historic bar, but also you can order contemporary cuisine or hearty "classic Berghoff favorites" prepared by the old restaurant's longtime chef in the familiar oak-paneled dining room.

What's different? The menu and décor have been updated to give the rooms a more contemporary European bistro flair while maintaining their historic integrity. But perhaps the most noticeable changes are the new faces and a more casual style. Briefly, the decision—an admittedly difficult one—by the former owners to close their restaurant ended the employment of their longtime staff. When Carlyn moved in, she brought over her already experienced staff from Artistic Events.

As Macy's red stars began to dot Marshall Field's landscape in the summer of 2006, the announcement that Carson Pirie Scott would shutter its landmark store at the corner of State and Madison came as yet another sad blow. Like Field's, Carson's family-owned stores had been acquired by successively larger corporations in recent years. Their stores in Chicago suburbs and elsewhere were thriving, but the State Street store had not been performing well and was also in dire need of a major remodeling. Rather than invest more capital in the chain's flagship store, owner Bon-Ton Stores Inc. decided to close it in late February 2007.

The building that housed Carson's, an architectural treasure designed by Louis Sullivan, is owned by a private developer who had recently restored the building's magnificent exterior to its original appearance. As was the case with other buildings along State Street that had formerly housed department stores, the building was renamed Sullivan Center and the interior was to be redeveloped into a mix of several retail businesses on the lower floors and office space above.

In contrast to the loss of Field's, public reaction to Carson's closing was subdued because the company not only expected to remain in business as Carson's but was also actively seeking a downtown location (possibly north of the Chicago River) for a new though smaller flagship store. Historic preservation of the buildings that formerly housed Carson's and Marshall Field's is insured by their inclusion on the National Register of Historic Places.

So, whereas State Street boasted at least ten major department stores at one time, only two remained in mid-2007. Both clung to the hope that the Loop's evolution into a residential neighborhood would bring in more customers. On the other hand, a very small number of longtime Loop businesses including Berghoff, Italian Village, and the Palmer House Hilton were more successful at adapting to changing times, and with more of their traditions intact. The loss of downtown's venerable landmarks, however disappointing, reminds us to step up our efforts to preserve history and to appreciate what we still have.

All photography by Eric Bronsky except as noted.

Carson Pirie Scott celebrated its 100th Anniversary in 1954
(courtesy of the Chicago History Museum, ICHi-15065).

Carson's in February 2007, one week before closing.

Carson's main floor.

Carson's architecturally acclaimed rotunda entrance at the corner of State and Madison.

"There is that desire to go back
and recreate the past, but I think there
is a little bit of truth to the saying,
'You can never go home again.'"
Ann Roth

Interviewee Index

Jerome R. Butler
Former Architect, Commissioner of Public Works
and Commissioner of Aviation for the City of Chicago
214-216, 218, 239

Michael Demetrio
Attorney; Partner, Corboy and Demetrio; Former President,
Chicago Bar Association 178, 180-181

Jerry Field
College Professor; Former Publicist
92, 95

Marshall Field V
Civic Leader; Former Publisher, *Chicago Sun-Times*
222, 224, 236

Myles Jarrow
Former Manufacturing Company Owner; Transit Enthusiast
58, 74, 232

Gary T. Johnson
Attorney; President, Chicago History Museum
32, 137, 152-153, 166, 188, 191

Bernard Judge
Journalist; Former Publisher, Law Bulletin Publishing
Company and Editor, Emeritus, *Chicago Daily Law Bulletin*
84, 86, 192

Mary Robinson Kalista
College Professor
121, 122-129

George E. Kanary
Former Electrical Superintendent; Railroad Historian
29, 88, 91, 184

Mitch Markovitz
Professional Artist and Illustrator; Trainman
182

Robert Markovitz
Professional Artist and Illustrator
96

Kay Mayer
Civic Leader; Board Member, Chicago History Museum
76

James McDonough
Owner, McDonough Engineering; Former
Chicago Commissioner of Streets and Sanitation
173, 176, 228

Paul Meincke
Television Journalist; Reporter, WLS-TV, Channel 7
198-199

Josephine Baskin Minow
Civic Leader; Board Member, Chicago History Museum
60, 80, 82, 186

James O'Connor
Civic Leader; Former Chairman
of the Board, Commonwealth Edison
137, 160, 194-195, 234

Potter Palmer IV
Civic Leader; Board Member, Chicago History Museum
34, 98, 208, 216, 226

Ann Roth
Restaurateur; Owner, Don Roth's Blackhawk Restaurant
31, 114, 116, 248, 249

J. J. Sedelmaier
Owner, J.J. Sedelmaier Productions Inc.
Design and Animation Studio
11, 164, 166

David Welch
Restaurateur; Co-owner, Phil Smidt's Restaurant
168

Photo Index

1 N. State Building 83, 97, 210, 211
1 S. State (Carson Pirie Scott)
   Building 73, 246-248
17 (W. Randolph) Restaurant, The 175
17-19 E. Congress Building 106
23-39 E. Congress Building 106
111 E. Wacker Building 217, 220, 221
190 N. State Building 15, 203
190 S. LaSalle Building 227
333 N. Michigan Building 217
440-44 S. Clark St. Building 110
450 S. State Building (Gem Theatre) 107
452-54 S. State Building 108
456 S. State Building 108
504-12 S. Clark Building 110
500 S. Wells lunchroom 112
500-08 S. Franklin Building 112
500-510 S. State Building 109, 110
517-25 S. Wells Building 112

Adams Street 48, 71
Aerial photos 4, 26, 37, 54, 133, 140,
   166, 167
All-Nation Hobby Shop 185
Amtrak 233
Anne's Rendezvous Lounge 105
Anne's Restaurant 79
Apollo Theatre 78
Armistice Day 85
Around the Clock Coffee Shop 150
Art Institute 30, 45, 53, 133
Atlantic Hotel 149
Auditorium Building 30, 104

Babbette's Lounge 107
Bamboo Inn Restaurant 135
Baskin store 61
Benson Rixon store 40
Berghoff Restaurant 71, 244
Bilandic, Michael A. 210
Binyon's Restaurant 227
Blackhawk Restaurant 20, 115, 117,
   118, 119
Blackstone Theatre 193
Block 37 173, 213, 236
Bond clothing store 165
Boston Store 39
Boston Store Clock 39, 83, 85
BP Bridge 238
Brown, Les and his Band of
   Renown 118
Buckingham Fountain 238
Burlington Northern Railroad 233
Bus, Chicago Motor Coach Co. 18,
   90, 157
Bus, CTA 151, 156, 158, 159, 183,
   210, 217
Bus-only lane 158, 159
Butler, Jerome 219
Byrne, Jane M. 219, 225

Carson Pirie Scott & Co. 73, 246-248
Casalino, Denise 231
Century Room 244
Chicago Aurora & Elgin Railroad 135
Chicago Cultural Center 233
Chicago Fire Department 94
Chicago Motor Coach Co. 18, 90,
Chicago North Shore & Milwaukee
   Railroad 42, 134, 135
Chicago Public Library 145, 157

Chicago River Main Branch 4, 49, 52,
   54, 75, 140, 166, 167, 183, 217
Chicago River South Branch 4, 26,
   54, 111, 148, 167
Chicago South Shore & South Bend
   Railroad 41, 183, 233
Chicago Surface Lines 33, 34, 39, 40,
   54, 58, 63, 65, 75, 89, 90, 93, 99,
   149, 254, 256
Chicago Theatre 59, 131, 156, 212, 223
Chicago Transit Authority 40, 131,
   135, 151, 156, 158, 159, 183, 210,
   217, 239, 246
Christmas decorations 120, 123-132,
   237, 255
City Hall 33, 48, 151
Civic Center Plaza 151, 173
Civic Opera House 40, 55
Clark & Barlow Hardware Store 185
Clark Street 39, 48, 61, 75, 78, 149,
   229, 239
Clark Street Bridge 75, 166
Clark Theatre 135
Cloud Gate sculpture 237
Congress Cigar & Liquor Store 106
Congress Expressway 37, 148, 239
Congress Expressway Bridge 148, 167
Congress Street 104, 105,
Construction, bridges 48, 166
Construction, buildings 23, 46, 55,
   145, 147, 161, 225, 227
Construction, roadways 39, 139, 146,
   148, 205, 210, 220

Daley Center Plaza 151, 173
Daley, Eleanor 230
Daley, John 230
Daley, Margaret 230
Daley, Richard J. 173, 230
Daley, Richard M. 230, 231
Daley, William 230
Davis, Monique 231
Dearborn Street 16, 17, 132, 150
Dearborn Street Bridge 166
Dedication Ceremonies 154, 210, 219
DePaul Center 225
Don Roth's Blackhawk Restaurant
   20, 115, 117-120

Eastman Kodak store 115, 117
Eisenhower Expressway (see
   Congress Expressway)
Electroliner, North Shore Line 134, 135
Escalator, Goldblatt's store 225

Fair Store, The 23, 29, 50, 90, 132
Federal Building, old 71, 149
Fields, Sheldon "Shey" 9
Flo's Restaurant 175
Flowers, Mary 231
Ford Center for the Performing Arts
   17, 236
Formfit Company, The 112
Franklin/Orleans Bridge 42, 148
Fritzel's Restaurant 154

Garland Court 21
Garrick Theatre 78
de Gaulle, Charles Cavalcade 87
Gem Theatre 107
Goldblatt's department store 101,
   165, 169, 225
Grand Central Station 26, 37

Grant Park 53, 56, 146, 147, 233, 238
Grant Park Underground Garage 146,
   147, 233
Greyhound Bus Depot 161

Harold Washington Library 204, 227, 235
Harris Theatre 46
Harrison Hotel 39
Harrison Street 39
Henrici Restaurant 79, 81
Hillman's Food Store 158
Hoe Sai Gai Restaurant 81, 150
Hotel, men's SRO 109, 110, 229
Hubbard, Eddie 118

Illinois Central (IC) Air Rights 140, 219
Illinois Central (IC) Railroad 133, 140,
   146, 161
Inland Steel Building 132
Insurance Exchange Building 103,
   111, 148

Karoll's Men's Wear 190
Komiss women's store 158
Kresge, S.S. Co. 87
Kyser, Kay 119
Kyser's College of Musical
   Knowledge 118

"L" (elevated) 20, 39, 40, 111, 135,
   136, 167, 189, 196, 203, 239
"L" rapid transit trains 39, 40, 41, 42,
   72, 111, 135, 136, 227
"L" stations 104, 105, 114, 154, 185
Lake Shore Drive 140, 221
Lake Street 39, 185, 227
Lake Street "L" 40, 185, 227
LaSalle Hotel 48
LaSalle Street 48, 59
LaSalle Street Bridge 48, 166, 183
LaSalle Street Station 26, 37, 90
LaSalle Street Tunnel 59
LaSalle Theatre 99
Liggett's 70, 85, 87, 236
Lindy's Restaurant 78
London Guarantee Building 49, 217
Loop Gospel Mission 106
Loop Theatre 156
Louis on the Mall Café 212

Madison Street 85, 99, 185, 235
Mandel Brothers 83, 97
Marina City 14, 174, 177
Market Street 30, 40, 139
Market Street "L" Terminal 40
Marshall Field & Co. department
   store 31, 120, 123-131, 156, 159,
   170, 174, 175, 177, 187, 241, 243, 255
   Atrium 120, 241
   Candy Cane Lane 124, 125
   Clock 65, 93, 122, 131, 156, 159,
   174, 175, 187, 212, 236, 255
   Cozy Cloud Cottage 127-129
   Crystal Palace Ice Cream Parlor
   212
   Escalator display cases 125
   Main floor 120, 243
   Narcissus Room Fountain 129
   Tiffany dome 241
   Walnut Room Restaurant 120,
   130, 243
Marshall Field & Co. wholesale
   warehouse 48

McVicker's Theatre 47, 85
Merchandise Mart 42, 75, 139, 183
Metra Electric 233
Michigan Avenue 50, 51, 144, 145, 217,
   220, 221
Michigan Avenue Bridge 49, 217,
   220, 221
Michigan Boulevard 18, 19, 30, 45, 53,
   56, 133, 146, 147, 157
Millennium Park 237
Model, architectural scale 209, 219
Monroe Street 56
Monroe Street Viaduct 133
Morrison Hotel 99

Navy Pier 239
New York Central Railroad 90
North Shore Line 42, 134, 135
Northern Pacific Hotel 103
NorthWestern Station 37

One Financial Place 227
Ontra Cafeteria 20
Outer Drive East Apartments 140
Oriental Theatre 17, 77, 78, 200, 236
Osborne, Arthur E. 210, 219
Oxford Men's Shop 13

Pacific Garden Mission 229
Palace Theatre 77, 163
Palmer House (early) 34, 35
Palmer House Hilton 132
Pancake House diner 193
Parade 85, 87
Parking 40, 113, 146, 147, 148, 203,
   227, 229
Pawnshop 109, 229
Pennyland Arcade 108
Peter Pan Restaurant 71
Picasso sculpture 151, 173
Pink Poodle Lounge 109
Pixley & Ehlers Restaurant 145
Planters Hotel 135
Plato's Place Restaurant 161
Plymouth Court 227
Post Office, Main 148
Pritzker, Jay Pavilion 238
Prudential Building 41, 140, 145, 147,
   161, 183, 238

Quincy Street 40

Radio Doctors store 109
Randolph Street 16, 17, 77, 78,
   81, 144, 145, 150, 161, 175, 200,
   210, 236
Randolph Street Viaduct 140, 144, 145
Randolph Street Station 41, 183
Regal Hotel 109, 110
Reliance Building 190, 213
Rialto Theatre 62
River straightening, South Branch
   26, 54
Roney's Parking Service 113
Roosevelt Road 26
Roosevelt Theatre 93, 162
Ryan, George 231

Samors, Harry and Bessie 9
San Marco II sculpture 227
Santiago, Michael 244
Sculpture, outdoors 151, 173,
   227, 237

Sears department store
   (State & Van Buren) 66, 104
Sears department store
   (State & Madison) 235
Sears Tower 238, 239
Selwyn Theatre 46
Shanghai Restaurant 110
Shangri-La Restaurant 155
Sherman House Hotel 47, 161
Sherman Street 102
Skyline views 53, 56, 233, 238, 239
Shoppers Corner store 171, 200
South Shore Line 41, 183, 233
South Water Street 33, 48, 161
South Water Street Market 33
State of Illinois Building 227
State Lake Theatre 13, 14, 70, 94, 131,
   193, 223
State Street 14, 31, 33, 34, 39, 40, 54,
   62, 65, 66, 70, 83, 85, 87, 89, 90,
   93, 100, 104, 107, 123, 131, 154, 156,
   165, 170, 174, 177, 190, 200, 203,
   229, 235, 248
   State Street Bridge 33, 154,
   166, 254
   State Street Council 83, 212
   State Street Mall 203, 209, 210,
   211, 212, 213, 223, 255
   State Street Subway 40, 41,
   72, 93
Stop & Shop 158
Street lighting 20, 65, 100, 170, 177
Streetcar, Chicago Surface Lines 33,
   34, 39, 40, 54, 62, 65, 75, 89, 93,
   99, 148, 149, 254, 256
Streetcar, Chicago Transit Authority
   131, 135, 154, 156, 165,
Subway entrance 13, 165, 211, 213, 237

Thompson, James R. Center 227
Thompson, Patricia 230
Toffenetti Restaurant 161
Tynan's Restaurant 179, 181

Union Station 38, 132
United Artists Theatre 79, 236

Van Buren Street Bridge 111
Van Buren Street "L" 40, 134, 136, 189

Wabash Avenue 20, 30, 40, 54, 105,
   115, 117, 119
Wabash Avenue Bridge 54, 254
Wabash Avenue "L" 20, 39, 40, 105,
   134, 135
Wacker Drive, East/West 52, 54, 75,
   148, 220, 221, 231, 237, 254, 256
Wacker Drive, North/South 139, 148,
   167, 183
Walgreen's 48, 131, 156, 159, 170
Washington Street 30, 33, 61, 123,
   151, 158, 159
Wells Street 42, 48
Wells Street Bridge 42
Wieboldt's department store 210, 211
Wimpy's Restaurant 135
Window displays 73
Woolworth, F.W. Co. 89, 187, 210
Woods Theatre 47, 161
Wrigley Building 50, 51
Wurlitzer 30

Yes Yes Club Tavern 108

A

Abbott, Merriel Dancers 80
Adler, Dankmar 76
Albany Park 32, 92
Andy Frain Ushers 160
Aragon Ballroom 114
Around the World in Eighty Days 152
Art Deco Movement 68,
Art Institute of Chicago 58, 96, 153, 188, 206
Artistic Circles 226
Artistic Events 242
Auditorium Building 76
Auditorium Theatre 76
Avalon Theatre 86, 168
Avondale 32

B

B & O Station (Grand Central) 164
Bach, Ira 216
Baer's Treasure Chest 91
Bal Tabarin Club 76
Balaban, Barney 152
Balaban, John 92, 95
Balaban and Katz Theatres 44, 58, 92, 152
Bambi 160
Baskin Clothing Company 60
Baskin, Salem N. 60, 82
Bennett, Edward 30
Benny, Jack 80
Berghoff Café 245
Berghoff, Carlyn 242
Berghoff's 114, 160, 180, 199, 242, 245
Berman, Shelley 86, 96
Bilandic, Mayor Michael 206, 214, 228
Bismarck Hotel 44
Blackhawk, Don Roth's 76, 86, 114, 116, 153
Blackstone Hotel 44
Blackstone Theatre 192
Block 37 12, 116, 195, 198, 206, 215
Blue Note 86, 192
Boeing Corporation 224
Bolling, Henry 180
Bon Ton Stores 245
Bond's 206
"Booth Number One" 12
Border's Bookstore 12
Boston Store, The 76, 88, 143
Boulevard Room 160
Boys' Latin School 98
Bridgeport 88
Broadstreet's Men's Clothing Store 182
Budd Company 68
Buena Vista 95
Burnham Center 88
Burnham, Daniel 30, 102, 206
Burnham Plan (*Plan of Chicago, 1909*) 30, 44, 102, 143, 218
Butts, Frank 74
Byrne, Mayor Jane 188, 192, 207, 214, 215, 228

C

Candy Cane Lane 122
Capitol Theatre 168
Capone, Al 44
Carson-Baskin Advertising Agency 60,
Carson Pirie Scott & Company 12, 76, 80, 88, 114, 153, 186, 215, 245
Central Area Circulator 216
"Central Area Transit System" 216
Century of Progress, 1933 68, 74, 218
Charles A. Stevens Store 206
Chez Paree 95, 114
Chicago Bar Association (CBA) 180
Chicago Bar Association Library 180
Chicago City Hall 207
Chicago Cubs 198
Chicago Cultural Center 207
Chicago Department of Streets and Sanitation 176, 228
ChicagoFest 206, 207, 215
Chicago History Museum 188, 226
Chicago Historical Society 98, 153
Chicago Kent College of Law 178
Chicago Motor Coach 91
Chicago, North Shore & Milwaukee Railway 164
Chicago & Northwestern Railroad 152, 153, 182
Chicago Public Library-Main Branch 86, 152, 207
Chicago Public School System 74
Chicago River 24, 28, 36, 44, 164, 214
Chicago River Flood 228
Chicago Servicemen's Centers 69
Chicago Skyway 176
Chicago Sun-Times 92, 95, 222
Chicago Theatre 58, 76, 80, 82, 84, 91, 96, 98, 164, 198, 199, 207
Chicago Transit Authority (CTA) 69, 143, 192, 228, 232
Chicago Tribune 95, 160, 235
"Chicago 21" 234
Chicago White Sox 198
Christmas 76, 86, 121, 122, 152, 186, 214, 222
Christmas Narcissus Room Fountain 122
City of Chicago 234
City of Chicago Department of Public Works
"City Beautiful" Movement 218
Civic Opera House 178
Civic Opera Lounge 178
Clark, General Mark 92
Clark Theatre 84
Cleveland, Ohio 12
Clockwork Orange 192
Colby's Furniture Store 114
Comiskey Park 12, 198
Commercial Club of Chicago 30,
Commission on Chicago Landmarks 207
Commonwealth Edison 194, 234
Condominiums 228
Congress Expressway 102,
Continental Bank 32
Conway Building 88

Cook County Assistant State's Attorney 178
Corboy and Demetrio 178, 180
Cozy Cloud Cottage 122
"Culture Bus" 206

D

Daley Civic Center Plaza 216
Daley, Eleanor "Sis" 207
Daley, Mayor Richard J. 166, 176, 206, 207, 214, 215, 222, 224, 226, 228
Daley, Mayor Richard M. 176, 199, 207, 224, 228, 232
Daly, Joel 12
Davis Store 68
Dearborn Park 207, 214
Dearborn Station 164
Dearborn Subway 143
Deborah Jewish Boy's Club 91
Demetrio, George "Ty", Jr. 178, 180
Demetrio, Tom 178, 180
DeMet's 91
Democratic National Convention (1968) 172, 176, 226
DePaul University 191
Des Plaines 152
Dirty Dozen, The 168
Don the Beachcomber 153
Double R Bar Ranch 12

E

Edgewater 234
Eisenhower Expressway 102
Elfman, Joel 12
Elfman's 12
Empire Room 80, 98, 160
Erlanger Theatre 82
Esquire Theatre 98
Evanston 164, 178
Evanston Township High School 178
Exchange National Bank 32

F

Fair Store, The 76, 88, 114, 143
Federal Center Plaza 236
Fenwick High School 86
Field Building 32, 68
Field Museum of Natural History 58,
Fields, Shey 9
First National Bank of Chicago (Chase Bank) 32, 188
Fitzgerald, Joe 176
Flight of the Phoenix, The 178
Ford Theatre 234
Forest Park 152
Forum Cafeteria 160
Four Seasons Hotel 234
Francis Parker School 98
Frango Mints 76, 242
Friedman, Esther 82
Fritzel's 86, 91, 114, 160

G

Gene Siskel's Film Center 12
GI Bill 92, 234
Girls' Latin School 98
Godairs 98
Goldblatt Brothers Department Store 60, 68, 168, 206

"Golden Mile" 195
Goodman Theatre 76, 199, 234
Grand Central Station ("B&O" Railroad) 164
Grant Park 172, 199, 216
Great Chicago Fire 24, 28, 32, 102, 164
Great Depression, The 68, 69, 74, 142
Great Northern Theatre 82
Greenwood, Charlotte 96

H

Half Day 32
Halshammer, Karl 122
Harder, Frank 95
Harold Washington Library 208
Harris Theatre 76, 82, 96
Hart, Schaffner & Marx 60
Harvard Elementary School 96
Harvard Law School 188
Hellyer, Art 12
Hemsley Spear 178
Henrici's 80, 86, 91, 114, 160
Henry C. Lytton & Company ("The Hub") 60, 206
Hinky Dink's Bar 188
Holy Cross Parish 84
Humboldt Park 32

I

Illinois Center 172
Illinois Center Air Rights 172, 234
Illinois Central Railroad (IC) 28, 36, 38, 58, 84, 160, 164, 168, 172, 182, 216
IIT Chicago College of Law 178
Inland Steel Building 188
Italian Village 114, 160, 245
Ivanhoe Restaurant 95

J

Jack Cohen's Pawn Shop 12
James R. Thompson Center (State of Illinois Center) 199, 207
Jarrow Products 58
"Joel Daly and the Sundowners" 12
John Hancock Building 222
Johnny Lattner's Restaurant 180
Johnson, Tom 32
Joseph's Shoe Store 114

K

Kenwood 76
King Arthur's Pub 178, 181
King, Dr. Martin Luther Jr. 116, 172
Kotos, Bill 178, 180
Kranz's Candy Store 91, 184
Kresge's 68
Kroch's and Brentano's 153, 164
Kupcinet, Irv 12, 92, 95
Kup's Column 92

L

Lake Forest 226
Lake Meadows Shopping Center 184
Lake Michigan 36
Lakefront Ordinance 44
LaSalle Bank Building (Field Building) 68
LaSalle Hotel 44

"Golden Mile" col...
LaSalle Theatre 234
Lake Shore Drive 143
Lake Shore Drive "S" Curve 209, 214
LaSalle Street Station 164
LaSalle Hotel 143
Latin School 98
Leo Burnett Building 198
Leo High School 84
Leonard, Bill 95
Levy, Charlie 95
Lewis, Ramsey 86
Lieberman, Art 178
Lincoln Park Zoo 222
Lincoln Village Shopping Center 184
Linne School 32
Logan Square 32
London House 86, 192
Loop "L" 28, 36, 38, 69, 102, 191, 194, 195, 206, 207, 216
Loop Theatre 84
Lyric Opera House 114

M

MacArthur, General Douglas 84
Macy's 12, 186, 226. 242, 245
Maillard's Restaurant 76
Mandel Brothers Department Store 76, 80, 82, 88, 96, 143
Marienthal Brothers 86
Marina City 208
Marshall Field and Company 12, 76, 80, 82, 84, 88, 98, 114, 122, 152, 153, 160, 164, 168, 182, 184. 186,192, 206, 214, 222, 226, 242, 245
Maryland Hotel 192
Mass Transportation Magazine 74
Maurice L. Rothschild's ("The Hub") 60, 206
Maxwell Street 91
Mayer, Brown & Platt 188
Mayer, Meyer, Austrian and Platt 76
McCormick Place 198, 214, 216
McDonalds 184
McVickers Theatre 84
Merchandise Mart 216
Metra Electric Suburban Trains 38
Metropolitan Pier & Exposition Authority (MPEA) 215
Michael Reese Hospital 96
Michael Todd Cinestage 164, 192
Midway Airport 215
Millennium Building 199
Millennium Park 116, 168, 184, 188, 195, 209, 216, 222, 224
Milton, Al 95
Milwaukee Road Railroad 182
Minow, Newton 186
Mister Kelly's 86, 192
Modern Jazz Quartet 86
Montgomery Ward's 143, 206
Morrison Hotel 44
Mt. Prospect 152
Municipal Pier 69
Murdoch, Rupert 222
Museum of Science and Industry (Rosenwald Museum) 160. 242

N

Naess and Murphy 234
National Historic Preservation Act
    of 1966 207
Navy Pier 69, 184, 206, 209, 215,
    216, 224, 242
Near North Side 98, 192, 216, 234
Near South Side 234
Near West Side 199
Nettlehorst Elementary School 80
Newberry Library 86
New Year's Eve 12, 114
North Shore Line 182
Northwest Side 91, 234
Northwestern Station 152, 182
Northwestern University 82. 114, 186

O

Oak Park 86
Oakland 88
O'Connell's 88, 98, 160
O'Hare Airport 215, 224
Old Heidelberg 76, 80, 82, 184
Old Town 192
Ontra Cafeteria 88, 91
Orange Julius 12
Oriental Theatre 82, 84, 98, 164,198
Our Lady of Peace Parish 84

P

Palace Theatre 58, 82
Palmer House (Palmer House Hilton)
    34, 44, 80, 86, 98, 160, 208,
    226, 245
Palmer, Bertha 34, 98
Palmer, Potter 34, 98
Palmer, Potter III 343
Park Ridge 152, 153
Parker High School 96
Peerless Candies 76
Peninsula Hotel 234
Peterson, Eleanor 186
Pickwick Theatre 152
Pixley and Ehlers 84
Plato's Place 12
Plugged Nickel, The 192
Potter, Henry 92
Preview Lounge 91
Printer's Row 102, 207, 234
Prohibition Act of 1919 44,
Prohibition Act (Repealed) 69
Prudential Building 96, 168, 182,
    188, 198, 214

R

Railway Exchange Building 226
Ravenswood "L" 92
Regional Transportation Agency
    (RTA) 232
Renaissance Hotel 198
Rhodes Scholar 188
Richman Brothers 60
Ritz Carlton Hotel 234
Robinson, Lucile Ward 121, 122
Rock Island, Illinois 198
Rock Island Line 198
Roosevelt High School 92
Roosevelt Theatre 92, 98
Roosevelt University 76, 92, 95, 222

Rose Records 199
Roth, Don 114, 116
Roth, Otto 114
Rubloff, Arthur 195
Rush Street 168, 192

S

Sage, Gene 181
Sage's 181
St. Ignatius High School 160, 176
St. Peter's Church 180
St. Philip Neri 84
Samors, Bessie 9
Samors, Harry 9
Sandburg, Carl 25, 91
Sawyer, Mayor Eugene 207
School of the Art Institute 12,
    208, 222
Schubert Theater 76, 192
Sears, Roebuck and Company 68,
    206, 208
Sears Tower 222
Selwyn Theatre 76, 82
Senn High School 80
Shakespeare Theatre 234
Shay, Dorothy 98
Shangri-La 86, 114, 160
Shedd Aquarium 58,
Sherman House Hotel 44, 76, 86,
    114, 143
Siegel Cooper and Company 68
Sinclair Hotel 198
South Shore 84
South Shore Line 182
South Side 76, 84, 88, 168
Southtown Theatre 86
South Water Street Market 28, 44
Southwest Side 160
Staaleson, Svale 32
Standard Oil Building 222
Starbucks 191
State Bank of Chicago 32
State-Lake Theatre 12, 82, 84, 92,
    98, 164, 168, 198
State Street Council 192, 215
State Street Mall 116, 181, 186, 188,
    192, 195, 198, 208, 222, 228
State Street Subway 69
Steppenwolf Theatre 234
Stevens Hotel (Chicago Hilton and
    Towers) 44, 91, 160
Stevenson, U.S. Senator Adlai E., III 188
Stop and Shop 91
Stouffer's 114
Sullivan, Louis 245
Surf Theatre 98
Sutherland Hotel 192

T

Tad's $1.09 Steakhouse 184
Taste of Chicago 207
Temple, Shirley 96
Theatre District 199, 208
Thompson, Mayor William
    "Big Bill" 68
Tivoli Theatre 76
Toffenetti's 160
"Top of the Rock" 86, 168
Trader Vics 76, 86, 153

Trianon Ballroom 114
28 Shop 122
Tynan Demetrio, Catherine 180
Tynan's Restaurant 178, 180, 181

U

Uncle Mistletoe 86
Union Station 88, 164
United Artists Theatre 98
U.S. Army 92, 96, 188
USO Service Clubs 69, 74
University of Chicago 60, 74
University of Illinois Chicago 234
University of Illinois School of
    Architecture 214
University of Notre Dame 178

W

Wacker Drive 172
"Wacker's Manual" 218
Waikiki Harry's 95
Walgreen's 12, 68, 98, 168
Walnut Room, The 76, 86, 114, 122,
    160, 168, 222, 242
Washington, Mayor Harold 207, 214
Well of the Sea 86
West Route Superhighway 102
West Side 96, 172, 234
West Side Riots 172
West Town 32
White City 30,
Wieboldt's 12, 143, 206
Wimpy's 164
Winfrey, Oprah 12
WLS-TV, ABC-Channel 7 12, 198, 199
Woods Confectionary Stores 76
Woods Theatre 160
Woolworth's 68
Work Projects Administration
    (WPA) 69
World War II 74, 84, 96, 102,
World's Columbian Exposition of
    1893 28, 36,
Wright Junior College 92
Wrigley Building 182
Wrigley Field 12, 198

following pages
Wacker Drive looking east towards State and Wabash
c. 1930s (courtesy of the Chicago Transit Authority).

State Street Mall looking north from Madison.
c. 1980s (Courtesy of the Chicago Transit Authority)

Plaza at Wacker Drive and Wabash looking east.
c. 1930s (Courtesy of the Chicago Transit Authority)